continued

For volumes in the NCRLL Collection (edited by JoBeth Allen and Donna E. Alvermann) and the Practitioners Bookshelf Series
(edited by Celia Genishi and Donna E. Alvermann), as well as other titles in this series, please visit www.tcpress.com.

Language and Literacy Series, *continued*

TEACHING OUTSIDE the BOX but INSIDE the STANDARDS

Making Room for Dialogue

EDITED BY

BOB FECHO, MICHELLE FALTER, and XIAOLI HONG

Foreword by Meenoo Rami

TEACHERS COLLEGE PRESS
TEACHERS COLLEGE | COLUMBIA UNIVERSITY
NEW YORK AND LONDON

NATIONAL WRITING PROJECT
National Writing Project
Berkeley, CA

Published simultaneously by Teachers College Press, 1234 Amsterdam Avenue, New York, NY 10027 and the National Writing Project, 2105 Bancroft Way, Berkeley, CA 94720-1042.

Through its mission, the National Writing Project (NWP) focuses the knowledge, expertise, and leadership of our nation's educators on sustained efforts to help youth become successful writers and learners. NWP works in partnership with local Writing Project sites, located on nearly 200 university and college campuses, to provide high-quality professional development in schools, universities, libraries, museums, and after-school programs. NWP envisions a future where every person is an accomplished writer, engaged learner, and active participant in a digital, interconnected world.

Library of Congress Cataloging-in-Publication Data

Names: Fecho, Bob, editor of compilation. | Falter, Michelle, editor of compilation. | Hong, Xiaoli, editor of compilation.
Title: Teaching outside the box but inside the standards : making room for dialogue / edited by Bob Fecho, Michelle Falter, and Xiaoli Hong ; foreword by Meenoo Rami.
Description: New York, NY : Teachers College Press, 2016. | Series: Language and literacy series | Includes bibliographical references and index.
Identifiers: LCCN 2015031217|
    ISBN 9780807757482 (pbk. : alk. paper) |
    ISBN 9780807774557 (e-book)
Subjects: LCSH: Interaction analysis in education—United States. | Education—Standards—United States. | High school teaching—United States. | Student-centered learning—United States. | Education, Secondary—Aims and objectives—United States.
Classification: LCC LB1034 .T43 2015 | DDC 371.102/2—dc23
LC record available at http://lccn.loc.gov/2015031217

ISBN 978-0-8077-5748-2 (paper)
ISBN 978-0-8077-7455-7 (ebook)

Printed on acid-free paper
Manufactured in the United States of America

23 22 21 20 19 18 17 16   8 7 6 5 4 3 2 1

*This book is dedicated to the teachers who
daily work against the soul-deadening instruction
that comes from overzealous enforcement of
standards and narrow views of literacy learning.*

Contents

Foreword

In some ways, it feels surreal to be writing this Foreword for Bob Fecho. I first encountered his name in the 300-page reading packet provided to teachers participating in the Summer Institute at the Philadelphia Writing Project in 2010. His work and its impact in Philadelphia was the stuff of legend, and my thinking around teaching and learning was certainly shaped by his words at the time. I am thankful to get another chance to be shaped by the words that he, his co-editors, and the teacher-researchers have collected in this work.

This book could not come at a better time as teachers around the country try to navigate the realities of standardization and increasing complexities of a diverse classroom. Not only is the narrative of this struggle told through the eyes of Paige, Lisa, Ian, and Angela in compelling and thoughtful ways, it offers concrete hope as in how we might think about our own work. In a way, we can all find a version of ourselves in the words of these remarkable teacher leaders—they are grappling with the same things as many of the readers of this book. When you think about the core of what you're attempting to do in your work, you will find that, like you, "Paige, Lisa, Ian, and Angela were trying to teach and act in ways that mattered, had substance, showed empathy, and respected students."

In an accessible and thought-provoking narrative, these four teacher-researchers and the three teacher educators present an alternative view into the complexity of the classroom. They discuss the ways they've encountered wobble moments and how these moments of something significant in the classroom have pushed each of these teachers to delve deeper into their practices to find how to reach their students in new ways. These are moments that we've all experienced but at times have ignored in the classroom. By having read this book, you'll be better prepared for what to do with those incongruencies in the classroom. Additionally, at the end of each chapter, each teacher offers a Suggestions for Action section in which logical, do-able steps are provided for readers to enable reflection and reveal new insights into their own practice.

Above all, this book can teach us about the way we can begin to create conversations among researchers and practitioners. In past few years, I have started to share with more and more teachers about the ways we can begin to tell our stories and shape the narrative around teaching and learning. One of the ways that I recommend we do this work is by having more partnerships such as the one we see in this book between academic researchers and teachers in the classroom. The combination of having the knowledge co-built by these two groups of experts would make research applicable, give credibility to work, and incorporate the realities of the classroom into theories about education. I hope that teachers and researchers be will inspired by the example shown in this work and build connections to continue the conversations started here.

If you've recently picked up Brene Brown's new book Rising Strong, then you'll immediately recognize her own journey to becoming a research storyteller and embracing qualitative research methods, and how it connects to the way this work has tried to honor the teachers' lived experience. In this work, Brene mentions the Asaro Tribe of Indonesia and their beautiful saying: "Knowledge is only a rumor until it lives in the muscle." This book is living example of this idea and I hope it inspires your thinking around your practice.

—Meenoo Rami

Acknowledgments

All seven of us who participated in the creation of this book want to thank Emily Spangler and Karl Nyberg, our editors at Teachers College Press, for their faith in and support of our work. Their patience and insights have created an atmosphere around which we were able to thrive individually and as a team. In addition . . .

Ian Altman: I would like to thank two colleagues, David Ragsdale and Matthew Hicks, whose friendship, goodwill, and professional camaraderie have been invaluable over the years; student Elizabeth Garibay, who inspired a new direction and a new vision of moral value in my career; Johnny and Maddie, who see right through everything; and especially my wife, Cheryl Washburn, whose love and ability to put up with my orneriness defy reason and description.

Paige Cole: I want to thank the usual suspects. On the home front, Toby Cole for his patience, love, and unending support, as well as Pete and Frida for their constant vigilance and determination to get a walk at all cost. I am also indebted to Richard Rosch, for his gift with grammar and his willingness and ability to edit me. I would also like to thank my dear friend and teacher Vernon Thornsberry, who reminds me about the beauty and importance of trust in teaching and in life. Finally, thank you, Bob Fecho, the leader and lifeblood of this project. You continue to amaze me!

Angela Dean: I would like to thank the research team of this study and Red Clay Writing Project, without which this publication would not have happened; my students, who continually teach me; and my two biggest cheerleaders in life: my patient husband, Andy Dean, and my sweet mother, Caroline Bennett, who believe in me through all things, but especially when the voice of doubt seems loudest.

Michelle Falter: I want to thank my family, particularly my parents, for their continuous and loving support of all my endeavors; my cat, Oliver, for keeping me sane while I pursued my PhD; and all the students I have had the privilege of teaching over the years, who have made me a better teacher and person.

Bob Fecho: First I need to thank Angela, Ian, Lisa, Michelle, Paige, and Xiaoli for sticking through this nearly 5-year odyssey. I also want to thank cats dipi and Alice for insisting on head scratches while I was trying to type, thus forcing me to take much needed breaks from the keyboard. Most important, I thank Janette Hill, my life partner and academic colleague, who put up with my silences, moodiness, and rants, which is probably more than one person should ask of another.

Lisa Hall: I wish to thank Samuel and Matthew for their patience and tolerance of "Mom's writing time" and am even more grateful for their much-needed interventions when it was time to balance work with some fun.

Xiaoli Hong: I would like to thank my parents and my husband for their continuous support as I pursue my PhD degree. In addition, thank you to my committee members, particularly my adviser, Bob, who guided me through this journey with patience and encouragement.

Preface

Michelle Falter, Bob Fecho, and Xiaoli Hong

This study and volume actually started as a result of a developmental review of *Writing in the Dialogical Classroom* (Fecho, 2011b), a book that Bob wrote that profiled the dialogical projects 12 teachers did in their classrooms. One anonymous reviewer felt that the book needed to be more research based; he or she argued that it was too anecdotal. It was a thoughtful suggestion, but it wasn't the book that the series editor had framed for Bob when she issued the invitation, and it wasn't the book he had agreed to write. So Bob and his editor thanked the reviewer, but they largely disregarded the suggestion in bringing that book project to fruition.

Still, the idea of such a book made sense to Bob, and with the original writing project behind him, he set out to conduct a research study that illuminated what happens when teachers teach in dialogical ways within schools burdened with standardizing policy. In doing so, he contacted three of the teachers who were profiled in the above-mentioned book—Ian Altman, Paige Cole, and Angela Dean—and asked them if they were willing to become co-researchers in a study that would be collaborative from the ground up. The three teachers agreed, and along the way, the team invited two of Bob's doctoral students—Michelle Falter and Xiaoli Hong—to join. Eventually, Lisa Hall, also profiled in Bob's earlier book, rounded out the research team.

It is important to note that Bob had prior professional relationships with the four teachers involved in the study. He knew, via spending 18 intensive days with each of them as they participated in various summer institutes of the Red Clay Writing Project, that Paige, Lisa, Ian, and Angela were deeply committed to issues of social justice, school leadership, and inquiry-based instruction. Then, by profiling all four of them in his book dedicated to dialogical writing projects (2011b), Bob developed a deeper sense of how they put these intentions into practice, each in his or her own way, yet speaking to the core values of dialogical practice. Knowing the commitment of each of these teachers to such work, of their abilities to articulate the wonders and frustrations of their teaching practices, and of the complexities and ranges of their teaching contexts, Bob easily saw these teachers as the best ones with whom to construct this study.

INTRODUCING THE UNIVERSITY FOLKS

The stories, practices, and classrooms of Paige, Lisa, Ian, and Angela that you'll encounter in subsequent chapters are the heart of this book. Consequently, you will come to know a great deal about what they believe as teachers, how they enact their beliefs, and the concerns they confront as caring educators. Undoubtedly, you'll get to know each of them fairly well. However, we three from the university—Michelle, Xiaoli, and Bob—are those shadowy figures behind the scenes. Not wishing to remain invisible, we think it's important that you have a deeper sense of who we are, given that the teachers' stories are filtered as much through our perspectives as through theirs.

In Michelle's Words

Before starting doctoral work at the University of Georgia, I had been a middle and high school English teacher for 10 years. My teaching experience in a public suburban high school in southeast Wisconsin, a bilingual private K–12 school in the Dominican Republic, and an international K–12 school in Germany gave me multiple opportunities to reflect on the varying and often conflicting notions of teaching and learning writ large.

One of my favorite units was teaching juniors how to write application essays for admittance to college. One essay example I had them read contained an ingenious use of the Pepperidge Farms Goldfish box graphic. On the original 1970s packaging of Goldfish, the graphic included a school of fish, but one fish decides to turn away from the rest of its friends and heads in a different direction. The student argued that she was a person who didn't swim with the crowd; she went against the currents and became her own person—a leader and an individual.

For me, this essay is more than just a great mentor text for creativity in writing; it also represents the task that teachers are faced with in today's educational climate. As more and more testing and standardization happens in schools, teachers are metaphorically and literally swimming upstream against rough and exhausting currents that are leading the focus away from the individual and more toward the common. Perhaps this is why you can no longer purchase Goldfish cracker boxes with this graphic. Today all the fish are swimming in one direction.

The question for me is whether the common direction is "the one" we want to take. It is my hope that this book can help teachers see that educational reform can support teachers taking their own paths that lead to the same destination—increased student success in the classroom.

In Xiaoli's Words

I joined Bob's research project the first year I came to the United States for my doctoral study. Coming from China, a country with a long history of standardized tests, a history that can be dated back to ancient China, I was surprised to know that American schools are heading toward standardized testing on the national level. This distressed me because the critics of standardized testing in China have pointed to many negative consequences of such assessment. In China, test scores in the College Entrance Exam are the only way to decide which university students get to attend; thus high school curricula revolve around preparing for the exam and students do a great deal of rote learning and memorization that strangles their creativity and critical thinking. Additionally, the whole society seems to be driven by the scores. Parents pay large sums of money for their children's extracurricular preparation classes and teachers' salary and professional titles are dictated by the college admission rate of their students.

Along with many educators in China, I saw standardized testing as problematic and felt extremely sad whenever I watched students pulling suitcases full of books on their way to school. I became disturbed when reading news about the collapse of a family caused by a child's failure in the College Entrance Exam. I continue to wonder who really cares about students' growth in the operation of educational systems that are rooted in standardized tests. Yet what the four teachers did with their students in this research project enables me to find hope for heart-to-heart communication between teachers and students.

In Bob's Words

Having taught at comprehensive secondary schools in Philadelphia for 24 years, I was also active as a teacher consultant with the Philadelphia Writing Project. For the past 17 years, I have been a teacher educator with a focus on adolescent literacy, sociocultural issues, teacher research, and, not surprisingly, dialogical teaching practice. In addition, I was a co-director of the Red Clay Writing Project.

As I reflected across the many years I have been an educator, I worried that too often the trunk swings the elephant and that what counts as reform lately is only re-establishing the status quo. I remembered being at a meeting in Philadelphia where a speaker was trying to rally teachers around reform efforts. The speaker kept announcing, "We're gonna turn this school district around." However, the image this phrase conjured for me was of a gang of laborers trying to get an enormous rock slab mounted on a pivot into motion. As the laborers struggled to push the heavy burden, they managed to break the inertia and get the slab moving. Slowly and with a creaking of gears, the slab inched forward until finally, with a great heave, the laborers sent the stone swinging, only to have it come full circle and smack them in the butts. My hope is that, by coupling the Common Core State Standards to dialogical teaching practice, reform can be effected that will launch the stone off its pivot and educational stakeholders will no longer have to look over their shoulders.

THE STORY OF OUR STUDY IN BRIEF

At the beginning of our study, the research team met at the aptly named Two Story coffee shop in Athens, Georgia, to discuss what this study was about, what our questions were, and how we would begin to do this research work. Together we discussed the power of story as a way to make meaning of our lives (Bruner, 2004; Clandinin & Connelly, 2000; Coles, 1989). We talked about how stories give us insight into the ways we construct and position ourselves in relation to figured worlds (Holland, Lachicotte, Skinner, & Cain, 1998) around us. Eventually the discussion shifted to how, through the telling and retelling of story, we either more reify or more diversify the story and thereby affect our ongoing identity construction (Hermans & Kempen, 1993).

The use of stories became our primary data collection tool (for a fuller description of our research process, particularly our oral inquiry process, or OIP, see Appendixes A and B). Paige, Lisa, Ian, and Angela spent the better part of a school year writing about key events that occurred in their attempts at dialogical practice within the policy frameworks of their respective schools. We came to call these short descriptive pieces "wobble moments," times when we called our belief systems into question. At a pace of two to three entries a month, the teachers reflected on how they decided what to teach, how to approach the chosen subject matter, and how they negotiated those decisions with educational stakeholders. We, as a seven-member research team, would meet monthly and run the selected stories through an OIP we developed that was based on work by Patricia Carini (Himley with Carini, 2000). It was through this collaborative and dialogical process that we were able to unpack the tensions and develop the understandings that we will detail in the remainder of the book.

Collaborative research is an amazingly complicated venture. Just getting to the point of starting a study involving K–12 teachers, doctoral students, and a teacher educator requires resolve and hope. The process of getting permission for the work from the university's internal review board, four school districts, and four high schools seemed to stretch endlessly. The lives of teachers are incredibly busy and emotionally full; taking the time to write and meet about their experiences almost was too much to ask. Coordinating meeting times put several web-based calendar programs to the test.

Still, we as a group somehow managed the writing, the monthly meetings, and the online discussions. As we told and reflected on the stories in our OIP, we realized that the process itself leaned toward the dialogical side of the spectrum. The stories that Paige, Lisa, Ian, and Angela shared prompted other stories about our own teaching experiences. These stories made the data richer and provided consonance and dissonance. Through them, we drew connections to other classrooms in other spaces. And, importantly, Paige, Lisa, Ian, and Angela saw their classrooms and their teaching practices through the eyes of others. In doing so, these four teachers could imagine other ways of understanding what had occurred there.

As you read the chapters written by Paige, Lisa, Ian, and Angela, remember that you are seeing but a snapshot into their working lives. Given that, we ask readers to understand that all teaching practice is messy and that options chosen by teachers at a specific place and time might not be the same options chosen by others, or even chosen by these same teachers if faced with similar situations in the future. In particular, keep in mind that we focused on the classroom events discussed in these chapters because, rather than being shining examples of dialogical teaching practice, they call up the complexity of such work. It takes courage for teachers to risk their practice to anonymous others who, no matter how well we describe the context, will only be working with incomplete data. Such is the nature of all research.

TEACHING OUTSIDE the BOX but INSIDE the STANDARDS

CHAPTER 1

The Story of This Book

Bob Fecho, Michelle Falter, and Xiaoli Hong

IAN'S STORY

Ian Altman, a secondary teacher and English department head, was facilitating a reading and discussion of Chaim Potok's *The Chosen* (1967). The work was part of an ongoing dialogue around issues of culture, race, and social justice that included, among other selections, Steinbeck's *Of Mice and Men* (1993) and King's "Letter from a Birmingham Jail" (1963b). Ian reported that "things were going brilliantly," as he and the class moved into discussions about the story of Danny and Reuven, two Orthodox Jewish teens who found a kinship in Brooklyn. Ian picks up the narrative here:

Midway through our study of this book, on a Friday afternoon after class, five students lingered in my classroom giggling over something. They were three girls and two boys, all very bright kids. I overheard one of them say, "He looks Arab," and another respond, "No, he looks Jewish." I asked what they were giggling about, and one of them happily handed me a picture they had drawn, a caricature of one of the two boys, making him look stereotypically Jewish, with a huge nose, big unkempt curly hair, protruding lips, and a big head on a small body. It looked like something out of *Der Stürmer* [a weekly Nazi tabloid], circa 1938.

Some wellspring of feeling I had long since forgotten erupted in me, irrational and visceral. It was an indescribable hurt that made me feel my Jewishness in that low, brick-in-the-bottom-of-the-soul way that I hadn't really felt since middle school when I got into a fight with a 16-year-old 8th-grader who fancied himself a neo-Nazi skinhead: a pure, absolute, heavy, grief-laden, glass-walled alienation. As they looked at me expectantly, I put myself in order . . .

It is in such moments that all the possibility and complexity of an engaged dialogical practice comes forward. For Ian, the world of literature and the worlds belonging to his students and him transacted in ways both

1

interesting and worrisome. In this moment, Ian, as a teacher, is dangling in air, wanting to take the next step, but not sure of the footing, the path, the direction. The moment seems primed for a deepening dialogue, but it is also fraught with emotion and uncertainty as Ian tries to determine how best to dialogue across the gap between his feelings and those of his students. How might he respond? What will be the many understandings that Ian and his students could construct from that response?

PAIGE'S STORY

Consider another teacher in another context. At the time of our work, Paige Cole was teaching high school social studies in a Georgia county that was undergoing transition from mostly rural to more suburban. During a discussion of the creation of U.S. political parties and the complex relationships among John Adams, Thomas Jefferson, and Alexander Hamilton, the conversation shifted toward contemporary examples of the legacy of those earlier events. As Paige related:

We also engaged in what Michelle [Falter, a member of the research team who observed that day] called a *purposeful sidetracking* to discuss No Child Left Behind (NCLB; 2002), which related to our discussion of the Virginia and Kentucky resolutions through which the states sought to rule acts of Congress unconstitutional. Michelle and I attempted to answer student questions about how NCLB worked and how some would see it as unconstitutional. I think this side discussion lasted about 10 or 15 minutes of the 90-minute class and almost all the students seemed engaged and a majority of them were participating in the discussion by sharing opinions and asking questions. However, not all of them were engaged, as I found out later.

Afterward, Michelle and I talked about the class, which, I felt, was purposeful and energized, especially when you consider most of the class period was spent on Federalists and Jeffersonian Republicans. That night I received an email from a parent who said that her child told her we spent the entire class talking about NCLB and did not get to the material that we were going to have a quiz on in 2 days. Her child was struggling in my class. I would give a quick quiz and the entire class would make A's and B's and she would make a 50. Because she was struggling so, her mother and I had had frequent conversations and email exchanges.

In this moment, Paige confronts conflicting perceptions of what transpired in her classroom. On the one hand, she sought the freedom to explore ideas and concepts that occurred to her as she and her students unpacked complex material. In doing so, Paige seized what many would call a teach-able moment and improvised a dialogue based on what she was seeing and hearing as the lesson evolved. On the other hand, a concerned parent who was worried about her struggling daughter had difficulty understanding why Paige didn't just stick to the submitted lesson plan and complete a graphic organizer focused on content for the quiz. Somewhere within the crowded academic day, Paige was trying to resolve how these opposite expectations might generate a healthy and productive space for learning. What, she wondered, do such tensions mean for her ongoing teaching practice?

ANGELA'S STORY

We now add a third teacher to the mix. Angela Dean, a secondary English teacher in a large comprehensive high school, selects the literature her students read according to an overarching question. One year, the question she pursued was this: What does it mean to be a citizen of the world? Teaching in a double-wide trailer—which was so long and narrow that it was more suitable for storing school supplies than for engaging students dialogically— Angela still managed to facilitate inquiry and dialogue regarding the overarching question and the texts she brought to bear on that question.

At one point in the early part of the year, she had students listen to two TED (Technology, Entertainment, Design) talks—one by Nigerian author Chimamanda Adichie (2009) that discusses how a single story can create stereotypical mindsets—and another by street artist JR (2011) on how art can change the world. Angela noted:

We had a terrific discussion the day prior on JR's speech. The kids engaged with one another, came to a consensus on their ideas about the speech, and then shifted smoothly into a whole-class discussion like they'd been doing this with me for weeks. This had actually been our first attempt at group discussion. I had a student sitting on the top of the back of his seat, trying to get in on the whole-class discussion as much as he physically could. Those who typically might sit silently and let others speak for them offered up their ideas. As the end of class came, the excitement of our discussion and what we'd just generated permeated the room and left smiles on most of our faces. I made sure to tell them how awesome they'd done and how well the discussion had gone.

Then came Friday. It just happened to be the very next day. Same groups. Same desks. Same kids. Different energy. I've got several who looked as though they were ready to shut down and go back to bed. Two girls were arguing over something that has nothing to do with the text. The boy in the group ducked his head to stay clear of their dispute. I kept coming over to provide proximity control only to find that I was distracting the other group sitting by the bickering girls. I tried to refocus them all and moved away. . . .

On the first day of the discussion, Angela and the class were energized and had momentum. She was hopeful that the time would be ripe for possibly shifting the class from discussion mode to some individual or small-group project that would facilitate their making of meaning. Then, perhaps while the energy and ideas were fresh, there might be a time to add layers of complexity and insight. But the bell rang; the students filtered out to the many individual destinations on their course rosters. By the time she and the class reconvened the next day, the students had shifted all the energy and engagement that they had originally focused on the class activities toward more personal ends. With the context so remarkably changed, what opportunities for a more engaged dialogue were left open to her? How might Angela pick up the threads of the day before and move forward dialogically? Was that even possible?

LISA'S STORY

Our final teacher, Lisa Hall, was teaching English in a middle school during the confrontation she describes below. The school, located in a growing suburb of Atlanta, had a large number of students who, thus far, hadn't had much success in school. Lisa opened her classroom to these students and it seems an understatement to say that she developed caring teacher-student relationships with them. One such relationship—with her student Emilio—figured large in making a mandatory staff meeting particularly uncomfortable. Lisa explained:

To try something "new" our facilitator asked four of our own failing students—academically underachieving and unmotivated boys, socially endowed in their own minds with "swag," and at risk for gang involvement—to visit with small groups of teachers and not only own their failures but also let us ask them questions about it.

Emilio was standing in the hallway outside our professional learning community (PLC) room when I put the pieces together. He was one of the four failing males and about to be led into the room of teachers when I stood up and said, "No. Not him. He won't be participating in this." The facilitator was annoyed and wanted a replacement immediately. My colleagues were a little stunned—people don't stop PLC meetings at our school. It was awkward, but I didn't care. I left, taking Emilio with me.

At first, Lisa complied with a process that on the surface had potential to be supportive of struggling students—the school team seemed poised to consider school life from the perspective of these students. However, in practice, the process sought to place the brunt of their lack of school success heavily on the shoulders of these young African American and Latino males. For her part, Lisa felt like the flag in a tug-of-war: She wanted to be seen as a team player by her colleagues and administration yet also wanted to advocate for her student. In this situation, she reflected later, where was the opportunity to dialogue? How could she raise her voice and that of her students into dialogue with the authoritative voice of the school?

OUR CONCERNS

Each of these teachers experienced what we call a wobble moment (Fecho, 2011a), one of countless such moments that occur in the careers of teachers. For a time, the equilibrium of their belief system—what counts for them as good teaching and how best to work with diverse groups of adolescents—is put into sway. When recognized either at the time they're occurring or later through reflection, such moments can prove invaluable in helping teachers refine and rethink their practices. Toward this intention, wobble moments signal that some event of significance is occurring and that it would serve a teacher's practice well to delve into such moments in order to consider new pathways and perspectives on practice.

Such systematic reflection is especially useful, as too many teachers in too many schools find themselves tugged between mandates to cover copious material in order to meet standards and their own experienced-based beliefs that urge them to teach in more engaging ways. As we on the research team discussed this book, the idea of double standards was raised, referring to this gap that exists between the direct instruction methods administrators too often expect teachers to use and the inquiry-based and dialogical ways most teachers know would provide for a more involving classroom experience. As such, many innovative and thoughtful teachers hold themselves to two sets of standards: one set imposed from the outside by federal, state, and local governments, the other a set of personal standards that, at least in our experience, far exceeds in scope and rigor those expressed by outside agencies. These creative teachers know that the systems within which they work will hold them accountable for whatever standards apply to their teaching context; but more important for them, they also know that they will hold themselves responsible for seeing that their students participate in learning that is richer, deeper, and more engaging than a rote addressing of the standards will allow.

To an extent, caring teachers live a kind of professional dichotomy. They know that teaching to merely meet standards is a shortsighted strategy, one that will leave too many students, especially those who have been marginalized by the process of education, woefully unprepared. That's why caring teachers often work in dialogical ways; it's an effort to interject nuance and generate multiple layers of thought into systems that are becoming too uniform. Still, these teachers also recognize that the standardized tests, checklists, and benchmarks will be there regardless of what they believe to be better ways to teach. Thus, they seek paths for dialogue within that framework.

Paige, Lisa, Ian, and Angela were trying to do just that: insert engaged dialogical practice within the testing-based and standardized policy framework that dominated their schools. In doing so, they were not unlike thousands of teachers within the United States and abroad who feel caught in the gray area between teaching the way they think will engage more students more often, and teaching within the narrow vision of literacy learning as established by federal policy and carried out by states and local school districts. This handing down of policy from the national to the local is akin to an oversized version of whistling down the lane, where an idea whispered into the ear of the first person in line gets wildly distorted by the time it gets to the last.

In all cases above, Paige, Lisa, Ian, and Angela were trying to teach and act in ways that mattered, had substance, showed empathy, and respected students. They were seeking to enact engaged classrooms where learning was more than meeting a standard, more than knowing how to take a test, more than satisfying a checklist, and more than placing a number two pencil in appropriate boxes on an answer sheet. Perhaps most important, they were taking responsibility for the teaching and learning in their classrooms rather than needing to be held accountable by outside evaluators.

Yet for these four teachers, engaged dialogical practice was more than a means for delivering instruction. Such a stance extends beyond the work teachers do with students, which is why we've opted for the word *practice* over *teaching*. As Paige, Lisa, Ian, and Angela sought to work in engaged, dialogical ways, they recognized the need to do so with the wide range of educational stakeholders. Difficult as it may have seemed at times, they tried to engage in dialogue with colleagues, with school staff, with administration, with parents, with business leaders, with policymakers, and with anyone who endeavored to invest in or impose control over public education.

As teachers, Paige, Lisa, Ian, and Angela aren't neophytes. They each have 7 or more years of teaching experience, have occupied positions of leadership both within and outside their schools, have multiple university degrees, are teacher consultants for the Red Clay site of the National

Writing Project, and have presented workshops and papers at national conferences. They are thoughtful and articulate teachers who routinely reflect on their practices and see those practices as constant sites of revision. Their classrooms are endless sources of data through which they routinely sift. They eschew the idea of best practice for one of mindful practice in a constant state of evolution. They think. They rethink. They revise.

Yet accomplished and as dedicated as they are, Paige, Lisa, Ian, and Angela are not immune to the fears and doubts that beset most teachers in most public schools. They worry that, despite their best efforts, students might fail standardized tests. They fret that if they slow down the curriculum to teach a complex concept well, they might not cover all the material they are expected to cover. They can't hide their concern for students who, already marginalized by class, racial, or sexual politics, are further marginalized by school policy, curriculum, and instruction. Like other teachers, they are disconcerted by those administrators who care more about seeing what standards are addressed daily than they care about the academic context within which those standards are being taught. Worse yet, they have become discouraged by the ways standards have become ends in themselves, eclipsing all subject matter, skills, and areas of interest not covered within their scope.

These fears and worries are fed by what we characterize as an overzealous push for standardization and accountability. With all the emphasis on getting this new round of standards in place, educators and policymakers often ignore data that indicates that standards alone do not reform make. As the *2012 Brown Center Report on American Education* (Loveless, 2012) succinctly states, "Despite all the money and efforts devoted to developing the Common Core State Standards . . . the study foresees little to no impact on student learning." The report goes on to indicate that past performance of state standards—be they considered rigorous or weak—has done little to change National Assessment of Educational Progress (NAEP) scores, which remain fairly constant. If other factors such as delivery of instruction, equity in funding, and variances in school quality are not factored into reform efforts (National Association for the Education of Young Children, 2011), we argue, any iteration of standards will be ineffective at best.

A concern for all of us involved with this book is that, as the nation rushes to adopt—or, in some cases, unadopt—the Common Core State Standards (CCSS) and the publisher-owned testing that will accompany them, substantive, thought-provoking instruction will be shunted aside. We worry that as inquiry-based and dialogical practices become even more uncommon than they already are, direct and rote-teaching methods will dominate and become what's truly common about the Common Core. Nor are standards or the influence of the CCSS disappearing from those states that have either never adopted or eventually unadopted the CCSS. Instead, as recent news reports indicated, the local standards of these states usually mimic, when not outright copying, those in the CCSS (Bidwell, 2014).

Of greatest importance, we question the implications of such standardized teaching for students and parents, and particularly those families for whom success in school and inclusion in the dominant mainstream has been elusive. What does teaching that is closer to test training than to critical education mean for Ian's undocumented students as they navigate a political system stacked against them; Paige's working-class, rural students, who often fall between the cracks; and Angela and Lisa's Latino and African American students, who are over-represented in the general education tracks at their respective schools? With the move to standards has come standardization, which means that instruction in too many schools is geared toward only meeting the standards and passing the test, frequently by any means necessary.

OUR PURPOSE

Our intent was to write this book from a sense of possibility and provide viable approaches and insights that enable teachers to imagine a practice in standardized schools that is more and not less dialogical. Each of these wobble moments that became the focus of our work, although complicated and knotty, offers opportunities for enriching dialogue. We also fervently believe that there is nothing antithetical about standards and engaged dialogical practice. To the contrary, we argue that standards that are performance based and leave room for local interpretation actually provide an excellent platform from which vibrant dialogical practices can be launched.

That positive stance noted, we are also realists and have experienced and witnessed too many well-meaning initiatives get used badly. The handle of a screwdriver might eventually drive a nail, but it'll take longer than using a hammer, chew up both the nail and the handle, and exhaust the user. Such is often the case with the implementation of standards. As concerned teachers and researchers, we have seen too many schools resort to soul-deadening delivery methods in the name of efficiency and standardization. Such tactics are especially true in those urban and rural communities hurt worst by the past recession and where the need for engaged education is the greatest.

If teachers find themselves in similar contexts in standardized public schools, they will need some guidance on how best to proceed. That's the intent of this book, to provide a focused examination of four secondary teachers trying to enact engaged, dialogical practices in schools where the CCSS and other standardization policies have dominated and continue to dominate curriculum, instruction, and assessment. By systematically and intently unpacking these wobble moments of Paige, Lisa, Ian, and Angela, we identify the play of tension in these contexts and consider the chutes and ladders that respectively undermine or support dialogical practices. Most important for us, we conclude by suggesting what engaged dialogical practice means for literacy education, especially in classrooms where the majority of students have been marginalized and disenfranchised by what currently passes as educational reform.

RECOGNIZING AND APPRECIATING WOBBLE

Imagine you're riding a bike and, after an unavoidable encounter with a pothole, you notice that your front tire is wobbling. Or you're entertaining your preschool niece and the wooden top you're spinning starts to wobble as it slows. Maybe you're perched under a tree limb watching dark clouds rolling in when a sharp breeze sets the large branch above you to swaying. It is in these wobble moments when you realize attention must be paid, possibilities must be considered, and thought given.

Wobble is not change, at least not in any significant way. Instead, wobble is an indicator that significant change might be occurring—often happening between two opposing tensions—and has potentiality to continue doing so. For example, if the flag that marks the center of a rope used in a tug-of-war contest starts to wobble, one side or the other is gaining momentum and change is being signaled. The flag may continue to hover somewhat near center or it might shift dramatically to one side or the other.

Nor is significant change necessarily a 180-degree shift from what once was. Most change is gradual and subtle, rarely cataclysmic. If that tug-of-war flag moves only a few inches, it's still changing position and such a shift is significant. The context is different from what it was even seconds ago and the team from which the flag has shifted had better take note before larger change occurs. Similarly, teachers who develop deeper understandings of what they believe or have a greater sense of other perspectives, even if they still disagree with those perspectives, are in the midst of significant change.

As social psychologists Hubert Hermans and Agnieszka Hermans-Konopka (2010) remind us, wobble moments can fill us with dread or open us to exciting possibilities. Too often in such moments, especially if we are new to a context, we give in to the dread and act in ways that remove us from the uncertain state, but don't necessarily change the context that created the wobble and uncertainty in the first place. For example, if a student were to say, "All women are whores," during a class discussion, some teachers, and some teacher educators, would simply proclaim that such views are inappropriate in the classroom. Doing so may end similar statements being expressed in the future—or may not—but, most likely, the student will take no steps to examine the misogyny of his statement, the class will have no opportunity to share multiple perspectives, and the teacher will have no understanding of why this student believes what he believes. In effect, the complexity of the context will change little, save to quash dialogue.

Hermans and Hermans-Konopka (2010) argue, and we agree, that when faced with the wobble caused by uncertainty, people should dialogue through the uncertainty. As difficult and volatile a discussion about misogyny with adolescents may feel at the start, it, at least through our collective experience, becomes a means for youth and teachers to encounter their own wobble and begin to layer and nuance perspectives that are often too set, simplified, and unexamined. By engaging that which makes us wobble, we take a degree of agency in terms of making future understandings more complex and varied.

ENGAGED DIALOGICAL PRACTICE

In Bob's kitchen, there is a refrigerator magnet that proclaims, "Warning: Perception requires involvement." Those of us in education who hew to what we have come to call *engaged dialogical practice* would do well to heed that warning. Such a stance insists that all involved be present, be aware, be open, be critical, be flexible, and be engaged. There should be no passive participants in an engaged dialogical classroom. If we are to perceive and, through that perception, make meaning, then we must be more than inert receptors of stimuli. Instead, engaging through dialogue carries expectations that those involved will put a premium on interpretation and response.

Although the remainder of the book will better illustrate what we mean by engaged dialogical practice, below are some acts of engagement that we'd like to see become more common, whether in a classroom, school hallway, principal's office, parent meeting, or school board meeting room.

- Seeking multiple perspectives during discussions and valuing well-informed arguments that go counter to consensus
- Nudging participants to not only question the beliefs of others but their own beliefs as well
- Providing opportunities and support for interpreting a wide range of what counts as text
- Viewing class, school, and community activities as interconnected dialogues that build on one another

- Creating opportunities for inquiry-based explorations that help participants unpack their own understandings
- Encouraging participants to develop meta-understandings of their own learning, writing, and thinking processes
- Supporting participants as they experience the tensions, uncertainty, and wobble that accompany engaged dialogical practice

What the activities above all share—besides their relative lack of inclusion in too many school district instructional strategy plans—is a stance that sees engaged dialogical practice as contextual, personal, social, and fluid.

Additionally, all the activities we've noted build on the language theories of Mikhail Bakhtin (1981, 1986). In particular, Bakhtin's (1981) theory of language is one that recognizes how we dialogically construct and understand ourselves through response. Words are "future-oriented" (p. 280), and therefore "understanding comes to fruition only in the response" (p. 282). Bakhtin argued that understanding and response are impossible without the other, that when engaged with language, all of us need to "relinquish the floor to the other or to make room for the other's active responsive understanding" (1986, p. 71). To be dialogical, according to Bakhtin, means to be open to response; it is through response that we begin to understand, learn, and grow.

Because our speech is dialogical, and future oriented toward our responsive listeners, a person may "realize [her- or himself] initially through others" (Bakhtin, 1986, p. 138). Bakhtin's notions of our sense of self as constructed through the responsive and dialogical nature of language are helpful in thinking about engaged dialogical practice. He wrote, "Truth is not born nor is it to be found inside the head of an individual person, it is born *between people* collectively searching for truth, in the process of their dialogical interaction" (1984, p. 110, emphasis added).

And this active engaging with and positioning toward response is what Paige, Lisa, Ian, and Angela attempted to do within their classrooms and schools. Put simply, these teachers and others like them try to create professional practice in which "literacy is used to immerse [all stakeholders] in an ongoing reflective conversation with the texts of their lives" (Fecho, 2011a, p. 8). Teaching that is inquiry based, critically oriented, and dialogical in intent is quite uncommon in U.S. public schools. It is the rare beast, made all the more beautiful, sadly, by its rarity. However, if the CCSS purports to be a set of standards that should be at the core of school curriculums, then we argue that engaged dialogical practice, as uncommon as it now may be, should be at the core of the instructional delivery of states and schools adopting the CCSS, or any standards.

FRAMING THE BOOK

Very often, people equate tension with negative connotations. We talk of tension headaches, of the tension being so thick you could cut it with a knife or stab it with a fork, of not being able to cope with all the tension. Yet without tension, so much of our world would not exist. San Francisco's Golden Gate Bridge would fall into the bay without tension. Your walking upright down the street would be impossible. The tension of strings placed across the sound hole of a guitar allows all those blazing solos to be played by gifted musicians. Tension is at least partly responsible for the drama in dramas and the mystery in mysteries.

We argue that rather than eliminating tension from our lives—as if we could—we should recognize the tensions that exist, try to understand how we are transacting with those tensions, and then do what we can to seek equilibrium across them. It's not the tensions themselves that are the concern; it's disproportionality across tensions that creates issues. When one side of a tensional continuum becomes too dominant over the other, our realities either become too uniform or directed by others or they become too individualized and subsequently too disconnected from others. Which is why, when we as teachers detect wobble in any of the tensions present in our classrooms, we should recognize that a change in the equilibrium is imminent. How we respond is then entirely up to the context at that time, but respond we should.

Returning to the language theories of Mikhail Bakhtin (1981, 1986), to embrace his concepts about the ways language works in our lives is to embrace the inevitability of tension being present in those lives. He argued that language is continually beset by centripetal tensions, which are unifying but eventually reifying, and centrifugal tensions, which are individualizing but eventually disuniting. As the prior sentence implies, we need language to be both unified and individual. It's not a question of one force or the other; there should be relative equilibrium between the tensions.

Bakhtin (1981) calls these "links and interrelationships of the multiple social voices that collide at any given time in dialogue" (p. 263) *heteroglossia*, or other tongues. Language is never unitary; in fact it is "a borderland between oneself and the other" (p. 293) in which forces that attempt to unite and centralize are in dialogue with forces that attempt to decentralize and individualize. Subsequently, all that we construct through language is also never unitary and remains subject to opposing tensions.

In the heteroglossic environments that are schools and classrooms, these centripetal and centrifugal tensions are everywhere, regardless of the methods of instruction and assessment. Systematic and intentional observations of any classroom would permit identification of any number of tensions.

Through repeated readings and discussions of the wobble moments in the engaged dialogical practices of Paige, Lisa, Ian, and Angela, we have identified the following six tensions as the most prevalent and insistent:

- *Globalization and localization:* What happens when local communities more frequently encounter cultural and political perspectives that are more global and diverse?
- *The personal and the academic:* What happens when personal beliefs and ways of working engage with more uniform academic expectations?
- *The conflicting agendas of stakeholders:* What happens when the agendas of teachers, students, parents, and other stakeholders transact in classrooms?
- *The mainstream and the margins*: What happens when the codes of the dominant mainstream culture engage with a range of codes of those cultures marginalized by school?
- *The ethical and the legal:* What happens when teachers contemplate actions they consider ethical even though, according to state and federal law, the actions might be illegal?
- *The expedient and the desired:* What happens when the preferred way of teaching transacts with a need to teach quickly and often superficially in order to cover curriculum and meet standards?

Paige, Lisa, Ian, and Angela at various times throughout the year needed to pay attention to one, some, or all of these tensions. Events that had transpired in their classrooms had caused a certain amount of wobble in the equilibrium between the opposing forces, and conditions were ripe for tensions skewing to one side or the other.

This book invites you into our thoughts and processes of unpacking just what engaged dialogical practices look like in a standards-based classroom. We lay bare the challenges, tensions, and "aha" moments that occurred throughout this process. To that end, the next four chapters all have a similar structure and intent. Each teacher has taken one or two wobble moments that she or he reflected on through our Oral Inquiry Process (OIP; see Appendix B) and expanded that reflection with the intent of gaining deeper insight into her or his continuing dialogical practice. In particular, these chapters illustrate tensions listed above that the research team identified and make visible the productive and restrictive ways such tensions transact in classrooms. As you read through these chapters, consider the ways these tensions transacted with the practices used by Paige, Lisa, Ian, and Angela and the suggestions offered by the teachers for dialoging with them. Also feel free to identify other tensions beyond those we've indicated.

In the last chapter, we look across all the wobble moments we discussed, plus a few others not described in Chapters 2 through 5, and revisit these tensions with the intent of creating a deeper sense of how they transact with classroom practice. Specifically, we suggest how teachers and schools might dialogue through these tensions, especially as such dialogue can be viewed as a complement and expansion to the CCSS and other standards. Importantly, we argue that engaged dialogical practice, although it presents a complex proposition within standardized schools, also represents the best hope for students—both marginalized and mainstreamed—to embrace an education that positions them for their technological and globalized future.

CHAPTER 2

Paige's Story

Paige Schadek Cole

> Doublethink means the power of holding two contradictory beliefs in one's
> mind simultaneously, and accepting both of them.
>
> —George Orwell, *1984*

As a history teacher and a human being, I get tired of people, particularly students, making analogies to Nazis. For example, if someone is strict, she is called a Nazi. I have even heard indignant students from time to time claim that something is "just like Nazi Germany." I want to go on record as saying that asking for papers to be stapled in a certain way is not just like Nazi Germany.

I say this because I am now going to be guilty of a similar overuse of an analogy and connect what I am seeing in my teaching life to George Orwell's *1984*. I am sure there are some English teachers out there who are cringing at the thought of reading another writer pontificating on Big Brother, doublethink, the Thought Police, or other Orwellian dystopian elements in an institution, but I cannot help myself. After reading *1984* last summer—embarrassingly late, I must admit—I was somewhat glad that I had not read it until then. Earlier in my life, I may have missed the profundity of Orwell's vision or I would have not seen the connection with the current American educational system.

In particular, reading Orwell helped me to see that my confusion at times over what and how I'm supposed to teach is not entirely the result of my own deficits. Instead, I teach in a system that may be guilty of doublethink, or as the quotation says above, "holding two contradictory beliefs in one's mind simultaneously, and accepting both of them" (Orwell, 1950, p. 176). One only has to read Michael Apple's *Educating the "Right" Way* (2001) to get a sense of how state standards are used to advance a political agenda. In his book, Apple argued that state standards are not neutral but instead are very much part of a larger political agenda. This agenda is an example of doublethink. On the one hand, many policymakers aver that such standards are politically neutral yet on the other they are well aware that the standards simultaneously support a political purpose.

I have no doubt that doublethink plays out in other ways within my teaching context, as well as that of other teachers. I teach the standards, sometimes dogmatically, while simultaneously disagreeing with them and the ideology behind them. However, my attempts at creating a dialogical classroom help me to at times resist doublethink, as I will explain below.

It was in part my skepticism and eventually cynicism over standardization that led me to be open to practice a more dialogical classroom in the first place. I call it practicing because that is what it is for me, a practice. I have no prescriptive advice or grand vision. The dialogical classroom looks different for all those who practice it because it depends on the people and discourses present in the room. In fact, there are students who do not always want to engage in a dialogical classroom and claim that they would be better off if you just told them what to memorize.

I also cannot really speak to how you can pull off a dialogical classroom in a list of easy steps. In fact, as you will see below, it does not appear that I was always successful at it myself. I have only my own experiences, but I will somewhat reluctantly share some of those with you and later will probably be embarrassed that I did. However, the hope is that, through staying open and even vulnerable in my teaching, I will move beyond the tyranny of doublethink.

As a teacher, I struggle with what words I will say, the words students say to me, and the places and contexts these words come from. This struggle can be ideological and can help fuel the creative side of what is happening in the classroom. This struggle can also shut down dialogue and cause me to recoil. At times I wish I had more certainty or tunnel vision where I could tune out the discourses of others. I, of course, possess this ability to some extent or I would not survive in a classroom; however, I do think that "the importance of struggling with another's discourse, its influence in the history of an individual's coming to ideological consciousness, is enormous" (Bakhtin, 1981, p. 348). I have pretty much come to accept that the struggle is the best we get. The struggle with each other and our different, and at times competing, ideological frameworks, as well as the struggle within us, can be the antidote to doublethink.

Doublethink is what we get when we stop struggling. I am guilty of this too; many days go by when I unquestioningly engage in doublethink. It may take the form of being numb to homophobia I see in my classroom despite thinking of myself as someone who would not tolerate such attitudes, or maybe the form of putting aside thoughts that are inconvenient to me as I am going about my daily routine. Doublethink exists within me, but it is not the space where I want to reside. I will probably never be content with what I am doing in my classroom, ideologically or creatively, but I will also probably never be bored.

I am not idealistic and do not suspect that the doublethink will end or that there is a perfect utopian classroom out there. Nor do I think the dialogical classroom is for everyone or is even a model that should be employed throughout school systems across the country, though if some district wants to pay me a large consulting fee to help them do just that, I would not turn it down.

What I do know is that I am nearsighted. I have not been able to see much beyond my arms' reach since about 6th grade when I almost failed math because I thought no one in the room could see the board or what the teacher was doing up there. Of course that was not the case. My nearsightedness, or myopia, extends beyond my ocular impairment and is also a state of mind. Teaching in the same classroom every day creates the conditions for a kind of myopia, where the big picture is not always visible. The dialogical classroom is a tool to shift the field of vision and see more than what is right in front of me.

DIALOGING WITH DIVERGENT VIEWS

In the sections that follow, I am going to share a wobble moment that I wrote about while involved with the dialogical classroom project. The narrative deals with a female student who was having a difficult time with the material in my classroom and the resulting dialogues I had with her mother and myself. On that September day, Michelle Falter came to observe my class. Michelle was a doctoral student then who was tasked with observing me during the project so that we could essentially compare and cross-check what we were seeing in the classroom. I made sure that I had many varied activities that day, as most teachers do when we know we are having visitors. I wanted to make a good impression, and more important, I wanted her to see my students at their best. I should have known that I was setting myself up for trouble.

We began class that day reading Thomas Jefferson's inaugural address (Jefferson, 1801) and we used a protocol where we highlighted places in the text that gave us pause, made us question, or made us exclaim. This is called the *punctuation protocol*. I posted a reminder on the overhead with the protocol listed. The overarching lesson for the day focused on the differing and often contentious political philosophies of Thomas Jefferson, John Adams, and Alexander Hamilton.

We also engaged in what Michelle [Falter, a member of the research team who observed that day] called a "purposeful sidetracking" to discuss No Child Left Behind (NCLB), which related to our discussion of the Virginia and Kentucky resolutions through which the states sought to rule acts of Congress unconstitutional. Michelle and I attempted to answer student questions about how NCLB worked and how some would see it as unconstitutional. I think this side discussion lasted about 10 or 15 minutes of the 90-minute class. Almost all the students seemed engaged and a majority of them were participating in the discussion by sharing opinions and asking questions. However, not all of them were engaged, as I found out later.

Afterward, Michelle and I talked about the class, which, I felt, was purposeful and energized, especially when you consider most of the class period was spent on Federalists and Jeffersonian Republicans. That night I received an email from a parent who said that her child told her we spent the entire class talking about NCLB and did not get to the material that we were going to have a quiz on in 2 days. Her child was struggling in my class. I would give a quick quiz and the entire class would make A's and B's and she would make a 50. Because she was struggling so, her mother and I had had frequent conversations and email exchanges.

This was not the first time that her mother had called something I did into question, and it seemed to be a recurrent theme that she wanted to know why we would talk about current events in social studies class. I do not think that I am getting too off track or "holding court" but instead see the little diversions we take as the juicy stuff that keeps students engaged and involved in the more tedious elements of history. I was upset by this email but it helped to remind me that we are not all having the same experience in a classroom and even though I might think a class went well and that students were learning and contributing, this is not the case for everyone. [We have elected not to provide a verbatim transcription of the email in order to protect the privacy of both parent and student.]

I must point out that this parent email is an exception. I had never received an email like this before and nothing like it since. However, it points to larger issues that are worth addressing. What is valuable in a classroom? Do we trust teachers and their decisions about curriculum and instruction? Whose voices matter?

Working Through Defensiveness

As my questions suggest, the narrative above offers me a lot to think and write about. At first, I was defensive when I received the email from this parent calling into question what I was doing with class time. I know I should not have seen it this way, being a person who is working on being more dialogical, but if I am anything, it is human, and at first I felt threatened.

It was also vaguely reminiscent of the challenges Bob recounted in his book *Is This English?* (Fecho, 2004), where he described the way his teaching pushed the boundaries of a traditional English classroom, and some students, who even enjoyed all the writing and reading they were doing, still wondered if they were learning what they needed to know. Except now it was *Is This History?* My students and I were having discussions that were not standardized and were diverging from the idea of history as existing solely in the past, and I was being questioned about this choice.

I saw the catalyst of the parent email as the graphic organizer that I had intended to do as a summarizer with the class. The split-second decision to start class with it the next day as the opener for class that day had consequences. The student probably did not realize I was trying to take advantage of her classmates' interests in NCLB to connect to the historical debate about state versus federal power, but instead saw the photocopied "worksheet" as a legitimate task that was not attended to, and therefore I had not been an efficient manager of time. I see myself as conscientious, and, if anything, an overplanner, so my pride was injured when a parent did not see that attribute in me.

The email told one kind of story but did not get to what we did for the majority of that class. It did not mention that we had read and completed a textual analysis of Jefferson's inaugural address. The email did not touch on the discussion of the contentious relationship between Jefferson, Adams, and Hamilton. It did not refer to the fact that as a class we had detailed the fight between states and the federal government for supremacy. Instead, it focused on that graphic organizer that was incomplete. It did not matter that I had told the students we would complete the graphic organizer together at the start of the following class. It did not matter that the quiz was on Jefferson's inaugural, the relationship between Jefferson, Adams, and Hamilton, and finally the fight between state and federal authority. The parent had the evidence, and I was guilty of inefficiency.

Once my defensiveness wore off, I was able to look at the email in other ways. I saw a mother who was desperately trying to help her daughter, who had yet to pass even the most basic of quizzes. My student may have been longing for a list of things to memorize instead of a bunch of concepts and ideas that we were weaving together through discussions. A list could be easily taken home and reviewed piece by piece, whereas a discussion was a living thing that I could not package up. She may have been able to enjoy the discussion and the class in general if she hadn't been afraid of failing assessments. It is now clear to me that I was not meeting her needs as well as

I was meeting the needs of the students who were doing fine on assessments and wanted higher-level work.

The problem was partially that I was not differentiating enough to sufficiently meet the needs of this particular student. Where the majority of the students had the vocabulary down pat and would have been bored to death by reducing the material to vocabulary terms that we went over again and again, this student might have needed repetitive drilling of these terms. They could have all handled this repetition, but I made a decision to meet what I saw as the needs and interests of the majority of my students.

This incident illustrates how I, and all teachers, are confronted daily by what seems like a million little questions that require a million little ad hoc and context-based decisions. Is it possible or realistic to differentiate enough to serve a diverse group of learners? And how do we help students with different needs while keeping others engaged? The good news is that by employing a dialogical practice I have the best chance of keeping an awareness of the needs of students whom I may otherwise ignore or possibly not even see.

Resisting the Banking Model

Within this situation there was also a disconnection between what I think the study of history is and what the perception at large may be. This disconnect may have begun with my not making explicit for my students and parents my purpose in setting the tasks and my vision for the study of history. For example, maybe I had not made it clear that reading and discussing Jefferson's inaugural was, in my opinion, critical to students' understanding of the partisanship of the era. I am not sure that many people see the importance of primary source documents and instead think of history as objective-based and basic-recall kind of learning. Where I focus on the bones of history, the underlying concepts like political rivalry or state versus federal power, there are many people who focus on the minutiae. Spending a large part of class time reading and discussing a document like Jefferson's inaugural address could have been confusing to some students who might not have been sure what the point was or might not value the process of learning to read through textual analysis and discussion. This led me to further investigate the standards and my dialogical approach, which confronts traditional banking models of education.

In Georgia, the state standards for U.S. history have domains composed of discrete information as well as a section on information processing. The problem is that when you get to the state-required End of Course Test, there are a large number of questions on those explicit little pieces of information. There are definitely some questions that ask for information processing, but when many teachers see fact/recall, they tend to put their eggs in that basket. It is easy to know that you lectured on X, Y, or Z, but how do you know you did a good job teaching students to infer meaning from a primary source written in 1800?

I was recently at a teacher-training seminar run by a progressive group of educators. We were asked to draw on large sheets of butcher paper what learning looks like to us. All the teachers, after the normal grumbling about how we can't draw, went off to our spaces with paper and markers and began to work. We then posted the drawings around the room and engaged in a gallery walk, where we took in our different depictions.

After we had enough time to examine our work, we all returned to the big conference table and began to debrief. Most of us had included elements of experiential learning, of students or ourselves engaging in hands-on activities. My own picture was a kind of triptych of a person experiencing learning through action, thought, and reading. The commonalities of our pictures were not what was visible in all of them but what they were all missing. There were no teachers in any of the pictures. Here was a group of teachers, and when asked what learning looks like, not one had included a teacher.

I tell this story because I wonder what my students would draw. If I asked them what learning looks like, how many of them would draw a picture of a student filling in a graphic organizer along with a teacher standing at the front of a classroom? Most teachers I talk to do not believe that the best way to learn is through a lecture, but most of us do lecture in our teaching. Why does this persist? My best guess is that lecturing seems efficient. If we agree that many high schools are still working under the factory model of education, then we accept that the bell is what governs our lives. I am reminded of the scene in the 2010 film *Waiting for Superman* (Chilcott & Guggenheim, 2010) when the director unquestioningly presents the banking model of education (Freire, 1970) as the only educational model, and the teachers that master it, as demonstrated through test scores, as the best.

I think many of us have come to accept that the banking model lends itself to preparing students for standardized tests, but at what cost? What happens to you in the long run when you commit to teaching to the test above all else and the way you have to engage in doublethink to make it through the day? Paulo Freire (1970) described the role of the teacher in the banking model this way: "The teacher's task is to organize a process which already occurs spontaneously, to 'fill' the students by making deposits of information which he or she considers to constitute true knowledge" (p. 76).

This model of efficiency is so common that though I protest against it, I still engage in it from time to time. I do not have time in this chapter to go into much depth about this choice except to say that it feels robotic, or, as

Freire (1970) would say, "necrophiliac" (p. 77). This is because the banking model is "based on a mechanistic, static, naturalistic, spatialized view of consciousness, [and thus] it transforms students into receiving objects" (p. 77). I can only do it for so long before I question what it is I am doing altogether.

It might be safe to surmise that my student and her mother found my teaching practice to be disconnected from the banking model. And this disconnection was creating issues for this student. Here was a girl who was struggling with basic recall, not to mention bigger conceptual issues. I had to ask myself if I was doing what I should be doing to help her. This questioning is what keeps me revisiting and practicing the dialogical classroom.

Engaging Dialogical Practice

Dialogical teaching is harder to practice than the banking model. The dialogical classroom can be messy and, if done poorly, disastrous, as is the case with any instructional approach. And to correct a misconception, engaged dialogical teaching is not a free-for-all. There is planning, grading, and then struggling and questioning it all. I continually ask myself: Did I create a situation where students could learn? Is it even possible to create a situation where all students learn? During the dialogical classroom project, I became more aware of when I was creating a space for dialogue and when I was holding court. The room came alive when it was dialogical, but as the email in question pointed out, it may not have seemed meaningful for everyone.

Esteemed educator Sheridan Blau told a group of teachers at a seminar I attended, "Whatever you do to teach your students, they should do." So, when I was preparing to teach Jefferson's inaugural address and had to read and reread the document and then highlight and look up other people's interpretations of a line here or a phrasing there, it jumped out at me that my students should do this too. For the class that I described in the narrative, learning looked like the picture I drew at that aforementioned teacher training. It looked like students highlighting a tough text. It looked like students writing questions in the margins of that document and then discussing those questions with one another and then with me. It looked like students making connections between the political issues of 1800 and the political issues of today and asking questions. It looked like the way I learn.

But do all my students see this as learning? Blau also told us, "The more you understand, the more questions you have." This statement, though I believe it, is not exactly what many people want to hear. The more questions we have, the more uncertainty exists. More uncertainty may lead to more anxiety, and I think many of us want answers. Many of us want things to be quantifiable or measurable so we feel like we have some sense of control.

We are left vulnerable when we do not have it all figured out, that is, until we learn to live in a more dialogical space. We are also left with lots of work to do and this work goes beyond merely covering material.

Resisting Coverage

I am weary of entangling myself with one word, but I cannot help myself. The word that stood out to me throughout the parent email is *cover* or its varied forms: *coverage* and *covering*. I agree with Bakhtin (1981) that "no living word relates to its object in a singular way: between the word and its object, between the word and the speaking subject, there exists an elastic environment of other" (p. 276). This relationship we have with words is messy and at times impenetrable. I do not know exactly what was meant when this parent used the word *cover* repeatedly in her email.

As a student in a progressive college of education I was taught to avoid covering material in lieu of teaching. I learned to not even refer to the words *cover* or *coverage* in any teaching conversation. To cover something does not imply to teach it or to create an environment where something can be learned. Instead, to cover implies to conceal or to protect.

When I look back at the email, seeing the word *cover* staring at me makes my defensiveness go away even more. This parent never accused me of not teaching or even of her child not learning, but she accused me of not "covering" material. Language creates culture and this process is a contact sport. Coverage creates a classroom culture that is about attending to breadth over depth. That emphasis has consequences that I am not entirely comfortable with.

I have my moments when I stop "teaching" and start "covering" and when I do this, it comes from a place of fear, competitiveness, and pride. I am afraid that if I do not "cover" everything, I will get in trouble or be looked down upon by my peers or administrators. Even though it is not humanly possible to teach all the standards well, I sometimes opt for teaching all the standards in a mediocre way. I do this because I have an institutionally ingrained fear that my students will not do well, that I will be judged if they do not get good test scores, or I want to be able to say to my colleagues and administrators that I taught everything, in case I am held "accountable."

The problem with teaching some things well or creating a dialogical classroom versus just covering information is that it creates a fractured classroom where doublethink is the norm. I know good teaching means creating the conditions for learning to occur, but I also know that I have to "cover" information. Students will often resent when you "cover," whereas if you "covered" all the time, then they would come to accept it. I have found that when students know you can do it other ways, they usually want it those other ways, especially if those other ways ignite their imaginations. Of course you have the students who plead, "Can you just lecture? I am tired" or "Can you just lecture? I learn better when you just tell us." Those students crave the coverage.

RAISING MORE QUESTIONS

When I first saw the Common Core proposal for social studies, I was excited because it listed learning skills instead of learning discrete facts. I thought liberation from the standards and covering vast amounts of material was imminent and that we were going to shift the focus from rote learning to teaching students to think and process academically. I was hopeful that maybe we were backing away from an emphasis on evaluating students on their knowledge of discrete pieces of information toward historical thinking. I was also hopeful that we would focus more on writing. I was wrong.

There exists a situation in social studies where, sadly, writing or anything requiring original thought is too frequently minimized, the exception being advanced placement (AP) courses where writing is part of the assessment. I have worked with teachers who have looked administrators straight in the eye and said if the students are not assessed through writing, then they are not requiring their students to write in class at all. Assessment drives instruction; I have heard that a thousand times. When teachers do not create assessments, or even have access to them, and the assessments that are created are made up of pretty low-level questions, we get classrooms that cover and avoid writing.

We cover it all so we can at least say we did. Quantity not quality. Drill and kill. And guess what? At times it works. I have done it and can attest to that. Does it make me feel good? No, but it gets the minimal job done and I do not tend to draw any attention to myself. Why challenge orthodoxy? Look what happens to people who do. Spoiler alert: In case you are like me and avoided reading *1984* in high school, stop reading here because I am about to give away the end of the book. Poor Winston Smith, the protagonist in *1984*, was tortured and eventually killed for daring to question or even engage in critical thought; he risked being annihilated by the Thought Police, just so he could love.

I don't believe we are living in *1984*, at least not yet. But I do believe that fear has crept into our classrooms, but do we have to let it in? The poet Hafiz (1999) admonished us to seek better lodging than in the tawdry rooms that fear inhabits. Fear is not the room I would like to keep residing in, with worry being my only companion. How many of us are putting ourselves in our own prisons? How many times have I given up on a dialogue before even entering it? How much of this is fear based and what am I afraid of?

I believe that most educators, administrators, parents, and especially students want to see learners engaged in dialogue and passionate about what they are studying. I believe that if administrators had been in my classroom the day of the NCLB discussion, they would have been impressed by the high level of the student dialogue as well as the connections students were making. I also believe that even the best administrators are, like most of us, capable of Orwellian doublethinking. It is not entirely their fault. They are under tremendous pressure to deliver the goods, whatever those goods may be that day. Test scores, game scores, grants—they are always under the gun to meet some quantifiable standard. It almost takes someone with nothing to lose to not give in to the pressure.

Teachers can be dialogical and create classrooms that are alive without sacrificing good test scores, skirting expectations, and acting as subversives. However, if it is all about the test, then it will be hard to be dialogical. To be dialogical means you do not always know where things are going. You are leaving an opening; you may not finish that graphic organizer. To focus squarely on the test is to know what the end game is. If education is a game and gaming the system is what you are interested in, then a dialogical classroom is not for you. Engaged dialogical teaching means going beyond test scores, not ignoring them, but measuring your worth by other harder to define and harder to reach standards.

Standardization and a focus on what is supposedly "common" instead of our conflicts leads to a monologic classroom, or a classroom with a single voice dominating. To teach dialogically means to have conflict. Parker Palmer (1998) claimed that "conflict is the dynamic by which we test ideas in the open, in a communal effort to stretch each other and make better sense of the world" (p. 103). I believe in creating spaces where ideas are tested and where students raise real questions to make sense of their world. I think I, and all of us who seek an engaged dialogical practice, just have to learn to deal and live with the conflict a little better.

PAIGE'S SUGGESTIONS FOR ACTION

I was reluctant to write this section, because I am nervous to give anyone anything that reeks of clichéd platitudes or that sounds pedantic; however, there are some occupational hazards that I have confronted and can share, as well as suggestions to avoid them.

A prevalent occupational hazard in teaching history and government comes from the fact that I could lecture all day, and not only would this be accepted, I would also probably be considered hardworking by many parents, administrators, and even other teachers. The "sage on a stage" model of teaching (King, 1993) can lead to a worldview that everything I say is not only right but also more important than what other people think or say. One of the dangers in thinking this way is that instead of approaching parents and students with compassion, I run the risk of letting hubris and self-righteousness guide my interactions.

Here are some of the things that I have to constantly remind myself of in my teaching practice and in my interactions with students and parents:

- Embrace humility. I keep open the possibility that I am not at the center of an issue.
- Stop talking and ask questions. Many conflicts began when I did not take the time to ask more about where someone else was coming from or what it is they needed from a situation.
- Pause and take some deep breaths. Wait to send a controversial email or ask a challenging student to talk to you after class. Taking some time to cool down and reflect before reacting can mean the difference between a time-consuming and emotionally draining conflict and a discussion that could shine light on a situation.
- Accept that vulnerability comes with the territory of honest and powerful teaching. Vulnerability means sharing of oneself in a way that increases connection and hopefully is not manipulative or self-serving.
- Know and keep boundaries because vulnerability does not mean a relaxing of boundaries and letting students or teachers forget the realities of public school spaces. Students need to feel safe, as do teachers.
- Play the edges, by which I mean don't shy away from uncomfortable conversations or lessons, but engage with them until you are right outside your comfort zone. It is in this space where the most interesting and thought-provoking discussions occur. Find

the places where you are slightly uncomfortable, being careful to allow for sincere thoughts while not crossing a boundary of what is age or school appropriate.

- Do not let fear guide decisions. Fear can be healthy, but I find that it can quickly turn into paranoia. I recently had a congressman come speak to my class who has a reputation of making comments that are controversial. I was nervous about how my students would interact, but when I moved away from a fearful stance, I saw that it was an amazing opportunity to practice playing with edges.

In this work we all rely on instincts and we all get frustrated and even angry at times. This is normal, but it does not change the circumstances, in which parents overwhelmingly love and want the best for their children. As an educator, I also want the best for my students. I have found that when this wanting the best for students is a fundamental agreement between parent and teacher, everything else usually falls into place. However, when there are differing opinions of what is best, ideological camps sometimes get established and students get caught in the middle.

Throughout my career I worked with parents who were incredibly supportive of me and I owe it to these folks to not let their trust and vulnerability be drowned out by occasional misunderstandings. I try to stay committed to the idea that if I can allow for a little space before I decide that a parent is not on my side or a student is being a certain way, I create the possibility that there is more going on in a situation than I am allowing for in my narrative. This can be an exhausting position to take. I have to constantly work at withholding or at least suspending judgment. This could actually be my life's work and is possibly even beyond this life's work.

CHAPTER 3

Lisa's Story

Allisa Abraham Hall

I began my teaching career as a 7th-grade English language arts teacher, a position I enjoyed for 7 years. Thanks to my commitment to engaging my students in dialogue, creating welcoming learning spaces, and building strong student-teacher relationships, I had some things figured out when it came to teaching. My classroom ran smoothly most days. My students thrived academically. The only problem was I was becoming professionally restless and felt I needed a new challenge.

So I looked to high school for new context, and I secured a position as a 10th-grade English teacher at a high school within my district. I was excited about this new challenge, and I was thankful I could continue to work in the school system I called home. As I made this transition, I suspected I would likely rely on many of the aspects of dialogical teaching that had served me so well in my middle school career. I knew I would continue to have periodic conversations with myself as I reflected on ways to assess student knowledge. I would continue to dialogue with colleagues in my school and beyond as I learned to teach at the high school level. I'd talk with my students and learn from them as they learned from me.

What I hadn't imagined was how this same dialogical stance would put me in opposition to many of my high school colleagues. True, my strong relationship-building skills and reputation for creating powerful classroom communities with middle school students had got me in the high school door, but it also painted me as a nurturing lightweight among my new colleagues. I was "too soft" for allowing students a second chance to rewrite papers they had plagiarized. Colleagues referred to my students' character bag projects as puppets rather than a thoughtful visual representation of external and internal character analysis. I taught the graphic novel *Maus* (Spiegelman, 1986), instead of the district-recommended *Night* (Wiesel, 2000). Although both dealt thoughtfully and pointedly with the Holocaust, clearly, a "comic book" was not rigorous enough for high school students. Didn't I know that?

Somewhat shaken by this turn of events, I spent the summer after my first year as a high school English teacher in dialogue with myself. Reflection had always been a vital part of my practice as a middle school language arts teacher, and I needed its power more than ever. The jokes and snarky comments of my high school colleagues made me wonder if they'd much rather I returned to middle school, where they seemed to believe I clearly belonged. Only I didn't feel right in middle school anymore. What was I supposed to do?

I knew I needed to challenge myself professionally, and I wanted to learn how to teach at the high school level. I wanted to do better for my students, so I went back to the beginning. I asked myself the hard questions that had served me so well in the past: What did I do well? Where did I need to work? What did my students need that I missed? Particularly, what stood out to me about my middle school teaching that could best inform my work at the high school level?

As usual, creating this dialogue with my past experience held me in good stead for my future teaching. During this period of professional transition, I recollected, analyzed, and learned from a number of wobble moments. As I recount below, two particular instances—one with Kayla and another with Emilio, both students in my middle school classroom—gave me insight into the teacher I am and the teacher I want to continue to be. In both instances, I called on my emerging dialogical teaching practice to help me identify and make sense of the tensions I experienced.

LEARNING THROUGH KAYLA

As with most classroom teaching stories, this one begins with a student and a tough question. When I considered the shift from middle school to high school, I figured there would be a certain learning curve and I'd experience the anxiety with any new and challenging experience. What I didn't count on was the anxiety my middle school students experienced and expressed over my decision to change teaching positions. I suppose I assumed I would be the only person affected by the choice. However, that was not the case, and as a result, I questioned my decision and wobbled with my understandings of responsibility and commitment in student-teacher relationships.

I remember being in my classroom near the end of the school year . . .

Kayla stalks into 2nd period, drops her stuff on the desk with a thump, and faces me. She is visibly upset as she asks, "I heard you're going to high school. Are you really leaving?" Her tone is a mixture of accusation and disbelief. My heart breaks for her as I scramble for a gentle, yet honest, response.

"Yes. It's true. I was hoping to tell you myself, but I didn't get the chance."
I surely didn't. Only moments ago, I had broken the news to my 1st-period
7th-grade language arts class. My students had done a great deal of talking in
their 3- to 4-minute locker break, and news of my departure had got around in
record time.

Kayla's face fell, and she opened her mouth to speak, but nothing came
out. I waited, as I knew something was coming. Kayla never had trouble
expressing herself. This time, however, she stammered through it, making
every word count.

"But, you know, you're like, the nicest teacher in the 7th grade. Where am
I supposed to go now?"

And now I am at a loss for words. In a moment such as this, I suppose
I hope my students will remember me for something I taught them about
language arts or even life. I am baffled by her question of place.

"But Kayla, you're going to 8th grade next year. It's not like I would be your
teacher even if I stayed. I don't understand."

"I wanted to come and visit like the 8th graders do. How am I supposed to
do that now?"

And then I do understand. She's right. My classroom is more than a
place where I teach 7th-graders. It's a space routinely inhabited also by 8th-
graders—my students from the previous year. They come in the morning
before homeroom, between classes usually after lunch, and in the afternoon
during connection time. Not all of them. I usually can't tell who might pop
by—I only have about three steady regulars. They come to say hello, but many
times they just come and sit until I tell them it's time to go. Sometimes they
don't even speak to me; they simply sit.

This lost chance to return to my classroom was what was on Kayla's
mind. I imagine she perceived it as an earned reward that had been forcibly
taken or stripped away from her, as the hurt never left her eyes throughout
our conversation. I didn't know how to make it better for her, because I knew
the only thing she wanted to hear was the thing I couldn't and wouldn't say.
I was most certainly going on to high school. I didn't come to the decision
easily, but once that the decision was made, I wouldn't change my mind. I
was going, even though the going wasn't easy.

Competing Forces in the Same Room

What made this moment so difficult was that it made me realize how much
my students depend on me for stability in their school lives. It's not just
comfort; I give them a sense of security in the world of school. Yet here I
was, whisking away their refuge, seemingly, at least to Kayla, on a whim. I

know this assumption isn't true, but I try for a moment to step into Kayla's 13-year-old shoes. From her perspective, she had come to count on me and our community space in the classroom, but now she couldn't. And part of that community was the way former students engaged with my current students. In losing that opportunity, she felt let down, even betrayed.

I think about how much comfort she had likely taken from my presence in her life and the space of our classroom, and I also wonder how that played into her willingness to work in that space. I am plagued by self-doubt in this area. In fact, the first questions I always ask students when they tell me I'm a great teacher is, "What makes you think that? What did I teach you?" I could say that's just me in dialogue with my students about my practice, and at some level it is, but at the core, it's my worry and even fear that I'm nothing more than the nicest teacher in the 7th grade.

Kayla's comfort level is important to me, as I want all students to feel at ease and safe to risk themselves in my classroom as we work together. However, while it's important, comfort level smacks up against another strong belief I hold about powerful learning—the kind we hold on to for life—and that is the idea that we have to get uncomfortable, shake off the familiar, and challenge ourselves and our ways of thinking if we are to grow personally and professionally. Bob calls this uncomfortable thinking space our willingness to wobble as we question and wrestle with our belief systems (Fecho, 2011a). My commitment to engaging in this practice is a large part of what makes me well suited for dialogical teaching, but the tension created by this daily practice also makes it difficult to navigate the relationships and dynamics that make up the social world of my classroom.

I certainly thought about wobble when I reflected on this tense, uncomfortable moment with Kayla, but I also focused on our student-teacher relationship. I couldn't help it; our discussion about the importance of my classroom in her life wouldn't have been possible if we didn't have a strong bond of trust and mutual respect.

This engagement is intentional on my part. I commit to forming, building, and maintaining strong connections with my students every day, and this aspect of my teaching personality is another reason why dialogical teaching fits so well with my practice—I'm always in conversation with the students I teach. But it also creates potential for tension with colleagues and administrators.

For instance, a colleague once compared my style of teaching to sugar. I assumed this meant that he and the other teachers at our school delivered to our students the opposite—medicine—or real instruction. I perceived that he wasn't interested in discussing how learning could be fun, even sweet, and still remain rigorous, and I came away from the conversation feeling that my style was definitely different and obviously wrong. But instead of working with the tension and continuing the conversation, I shut down and stopped the dialogue. What I needed to do was keep talking, even if the conversation was an uncomfortable one.

As a result, the question of how much of the personal belongs in my classroom is never far from my mind, and I'm always wondering where and when I should draw the line between the personal and the academic within me. It's true I treasure the relationships I build with my students because the work that grows from our dialogue always feels very real and authentic. That's possible because dialogical practice has an amazing capacity for diminishing the hierarchies that set me apart from my students. Without it, I'm primarily a sage on the stage with the authority to assign grades and homework. Students may approach my desk if they dare.

However, with dialogical teaching in practice through our student-teacher relationship, the lines that separate us blur a bit. I'm more approachable, not simply because I'm an adult who knows about language arts, but because I'm willing to listen and learn from my students as well as share my knowledge with them. When Kayla questioned me about the rumor she had heard, she felt empowered and entitled to do so. Because we'd spent the year building our relationship, she felt comfortable enough to come straight to the source and ask me about what she had heard. Without our strong relationship, she might have decided that it wasn't her right to ask such questions, despite the impact on her. It's also possible she might not have cared enough to ask at all.

A Chance Encounter

As we talk from this place of risk-taking comfort, anything is possible, but it's precisely the limitlessness of these transactional possibilities that has the potential to make our relationship a sticky negotiation as well. With young teens, the dynamics of the relationship are constantly changing, almost day to day.

I recently had a former middle school student, Rayshawn, now a junior in high school, come visit and help me after school in my room. As we worked setting up headphones in the computer area, she recalled our roller-coaster student-teacher relationship, and I asked her to explain it from her perspective. She said, "I started out loving you, and then I hated you, and then I loved you again."

I asked Rayshawn why she thought that was so. Why the love-hate spectrum? "I don't know," she said, "but at the beginning, I could tell you cared about me, and that made me care for you, and then it seemed like I was always getting in trouble and you were on my case, and I hated you for it. Then, I guess, I went back to thinking you cared for me. So, I loved you back."

I didn't have a ready response for that. I thought about the frailty of human relationships and how a single response can shape opinion even if the intention is not there to do so. For Rayshawn, her interpretation of my tendency to "get on her case" allowed her to believe I didn't like her or didn't approve of her, so she felt her only course of action was to stop loving me altogether. Like Kayla, she depended on my encouragement in our student-teacher relationship in order to feel secure, but when Rayshawn perceived me to be "on her case," then her sense of stability was threatened.

This encounter made me think further about the power of words and how I wanted to make them count for good in students' lives. And I wondered if the love/hate dynamic I created with this student is part of the deal for dialogical teachers, as I've encountered it before with many others. Perhaps the feelings of hate were by-products of my nudging and prodding Rayshawn to take risks, try harder, do more, demand more of herself. I do know she moved on from my remedial reading class in the 7th grade to take AP language classes in high school. I can't take credit for her effort and risk, but I hope the dynamics of our student-teacher relationship at least provided her with the courage and motivation to try to make more rigorous choices in the future.

It made me understand how completely accessible students believe teachers must be at all times. For them, it's a non-negotiable expectation. So, in that sense, a dialogical teaching relationship can be a mentally draining and exhausting experience. Teachers must be prepared for that.

Moving Beyond the Wobble

I experienced a dynamic in my relationship with Kayla similar to that in my relationship with Rayshawn. Kayla and I didn't talk every day, and in truth, I was frequently on her case with reminders to do better work and the importance of making deadlines. I remembered more days where I was certain she hated my guts. Therefore, her intense reaction and distress caused by my departure took me entirely by surprise. My sudden discovery that Kayla cared for me deeply motivated me to write through the experience, reflect on what this meant for my teaching practice, and talk about it with other professionals.

Kayla's question not only made me pause; it haunted me as an educator. How many other students felt betrayed by my move to high school and were simply afraid to say so? On the other hand, how many were indifferent? It's true that students react differently to disruptions in routine. Some cry, some stop talking to us, others confront us, but what does that mean for us as educators? What are educators to do with this knowledge?

I questioned this disruption in my teaching practice. I worried about Kayla and others as I worked through some of my anxieties for them through writing, but ultimately, I had to learn something about myself as a teacher to make the process useful to my practice. So, I wondered, how did this relationship and others disrupt my ideas about teaching and make me think and wobble with my belief system?

I came to a deeper understanding of this question through the connections my colleagues on the research team made to the story I shared. One common thread reverberated in everyone's response—all were surprised and even shocked by the students who return to them. We *all* recalled students who presented immense behavior management problems showing up a year later looking for something, perhaps just a place to sit or some conversation. Every one of us expressed genuine surprise by these encounters and shock that anything positive had come from these particularly difficult student-teacher relationships.

We talked about the seemingly prevalent expectation across students for teachers to stand still in time, perhaps function as museum artifacts dedicated to childhood. We laughed about this teacher myth, the one where we actually sleep on rollout cots kept somewhere in the classroom. But we became more somber as we wondered when and if teachers ever get the freedom to be real people. We wondered if and when we'd know we'd reached a point where it would be necessary to cut ourselves off from our students in an effort to protect ourselves from burning out. We realized that we, as dialogical teachers, were more susceptible to this outcome as we engaged with our students more fully and regularly than did other educators.

I acknowledged the possibility of this consequence, but I also acknowledged how participating in rich dialogical relationships continually broadens the scope and depth of my understanding in terms of my classroom, my students, and my students' learning needs. Clearly, different students would always require different levels of engagement from me. For this reason continued dialogue becomes vital.

My reflection returned me to my foundational belief that true learning can't happen unless we are willing to make ourselves vulnerable and uncomfortable. The experience made me uneasy and demanded that I pay attention to it and similar ones in the future. It forced me to admit that even if I want to be accessible to students and strive to create welcoming environments for them while they are at school, many students will not respond to my invitation. As a dialogical teacher, I must pay attention to these silent spaces where students do not speak just as much as I attend to the students who reach out and connect to me and monopolize my time. The wobble moment forces me to understand that dialogical teaching is as much about listening as it is about exchanging words with another in dialogue.

LEARNING THROUGH EMILIO

A moment of wobble I experienced with another student, Emilio, is a powerful example of different students' requiring different levels of engagement from their teachers. As seems to be the case for my practice, the stronger the relationships I build with students are, the stronger my tendency is to care and attend to their needs, whether they be social or academic in nature. In this way, I function as an advocate for my students. Sometimes, however, such advocacy places me in opposition to school colleagues. Quite possibly this opposition might even prevent me from opening up dialogue with those colleagues—dialogue that in the end could result in even stronger advocacy for students in my school who remain marginalized by current policies and practices.

Such was the case with an incident that involved Emilio and a meeting of 7th-grade teachers at my school. At year's end, I reflected on my connection to this engaging student and how this connection colored the wobble moment that occurred in the grade group meeting . . .

I took three photographs with Emilio on the final day of school. In the last, we tried to look tough, at least I did. I wasn't very convincing with my turned-up collar and the stunned look in my eyes, whereas, Emilio—whom I always called Milio—didn't even have to try. Hood on and shoulders hunched a bit, his eyes speak years of experience my own White, privileged, and sheltered existence can't begin to fathom.

His arm is draped around my shoulder, his fingers splayed possessively, as if he is afraid to let go. It could be he does not know how to take formal pictures and compose his body properly, but I doubt that is the case. At 15, he is years older than my other 7th-grade students. The girls in class swoon over Milio just because of it. The boys want to hang with him so that his knowledge and experience will rub off on them and make them cool by mere association.

It was true—he was more mature than the other students—but I could always catch little glimpses of a wide-eyed, little boy wonder in Milio. It made him endearing. I still remember the look on his face when I shared a story from my junior high years with our 1st-period class. A boy had asked me to dance at the 8th-grade spring formal, then laughed at me and told me to have fun (dancing with myself, that is).

Emilio had chuckled along with his classmates as I recounted my tale of teenage angst, but his reaction was different in that he processed the slight on my behalf. It was interesting to watch it register on his face as he seemed to resolve in just a few seconds that the 8th-grade boy from my past was an absolute idiot. And in that moment, I loved Milio. Certainly not in a romantic way, but for the unspoken gesture and understanding that he would like to go back in time, beat up the boy to protect my honor, and spare me any unnecessary embarrassment.

I, too, would protect him from slight and embarrassment, and have. I remember a professional learning meeting where we were discussing the problem of failing males in our school. To try something "new," our facilitator asked four of our own failing students—academically underachieving and unmotivated boys, socially endowed in their own minds with "swag," and at risk for gang involvement—to visit with small groups of teachers and not only own their failures but also let us ask them questions about it.

Emilio was standing in the hallway outside our professional learning community (PLC) room when I put the pieces together. He was one of the four failing males and about to be led into the room of teachers when I stood up and said, "No. Not him. He won't be participating in this." The facilitator was annoyed and wanted a replacement immediately. My colleagues were a little stunned—people don't stop PLC meetings at our school. It was awkward, but I didn't care. I left, taking Emilio with me.

Making Meaning of a Wobble Moment

What followed my objection to Emilio's participation in the professional learning activity is not clearly etched into my memory. I know I removed Emilio from the room and walked him back to class. I returned to the meeting, which was proceeding without me, and sat in a small group. Another child had replaced Emilio, and my 7th-grade colleagues were asking him questions about school and engagement. I pretended to listen, but I resented every moment. The bell rang, and the meeting ended. I went back to my classroom without a word to the facilitator, but the experience weighed on my mind.

I was mad. Angry for Emilio, but upset at my colleagues, too. I couldn't forget how trapped I felt in that monologic space. How were the others content to participate in this humiliating process without a word? We never approached challenges as a 7th-grade team in such a timid manner, so I couldn't fathom their acquiescence now. Why was I the only one speaking up?

I was also angry about the agenda of the meeting. There was no invitation to discuss how we might approach or inquire into the problem of student failure in our school. It was simply a presentation from one faculty member to others. Everything was decided beforehand, right down to how we were to talk about it. The entire meeting was scripted and coming from one authoritative voice. The only way out, it seemed to me, was to push back and refuse.

The pushing back certainly placed me at odds with our meeting facilitator; I had disrupted the flow of the activity when others were participating without complaint. Clearly, she expected us to participate in the activity just as good team players do, so I wondered if my teammates resented my actions and wished I had just gone along for the sake of getting along.

At lunch that day I did talk about my resistance with my closest colleagues; they were supportive but said they were surprised by my actions. When a teammate pointed out how I intervened as a parent would, I noticed how he chose his words carefully and spoke deliberately, as if dealing with a delicate situation. Perhaps he believed my intervention was out of line but didn't want to hurt my feelings. Maybe he thought my response was too emotional. He never clarified his comment, and I never asked him to elaborate on what he meant.

I also never discussed my opposition to the activity with our professional learning facilitator, and many times I wish I had talked with her, for although I spoke up against the activity, I considered her a friend. Perhaps we might have grown something positive from the discord at that meeting and opened an opportunity to dialogue about reaching and teaching students in our school, but we didn't, and I believe that's what a dialogical teacher would do. As a result, it's likely nothing has changed about how that building's administration approaches such issues, and I regret not seizing the chance to open dialogue and start a discussion of how we might accomplish that change together.

My silence on that front forced me to stop and question my own commitment to engaged dialogical practice. It's true; I stood up, but only for Emilio. I didn't step in for the other boys, even though I understood the activity to be wrong and potentially damaging for students. One member on our research team point-blank asked me, "Why didn't you stop the activity for the other boys, too?" And I wondered what happened to the brave, bold lady so many of my friends and family have come to know. I felt weak in that moment when I had imagined myself as a powerful champion only seconds before. I even questioned my identification as a dialogical teacher, someone who I imagined would speak up for all the students and not just the ones she knew well and liked.

Thinking further about the meeting and my actions, I wondered if in writing about this wobble moment, I revealed myself as nothing more than a caring teacher who builds great relationships with her students. But isn't that a good characteristic, I wondered. The wobble moment surely identified my need to examine closely the tension between speaking up and keeping silent in education, really explore that sticky space of student advocate versus academic evaluator. As I continued to unpack this incident with colleagues, I confronted this tension in my work and thought about not only my silence in regard to the other three boys at the meeting but also what courage and strength was made possible through my dialogical teaching stance and my strong relationship with Emilio.

In truth, so many subject positions and possible stances influenced my response to the activity and my colleague. For instance, I needed to confront my timidity, but also back off the inclination to beat myself up. Here, I was in dialogue with myself, or at least in dialogue with my practice. For my ability to make decisions in the classroom and any response I made on behalf of Emilio is tied up in what Fecho and Botzakis (2007) called "an ongoing process." They go on, "Meaning is being made, but a meaning that remains dependent on the players and the playground" (p. 551). In other words, our actions in the moment are heavily influenced by context; in my case, the relationship created in the space of my classroom strongly influenced my reaction to others in the professional learning meeting.

Listening to others on the research team as they talked through the experience I shared here was helpful as it gave me a lens to see the wider landscape outside my classroom. Certainly, my strong relationship with Emilio made his feelings personal to me, and that is the reason I believe I stood up in that meeting and refused to allow his participation in our activity. What sharing the wobble moment did for me, however, was alert me to the fact that the issues specific to my classroom are present in classrooms everywhere and require not only my vigilant attention but also the attention of all teachers.

Students are exposed to potential ridicule every day in a variety of contexts. It is not wrong to stand up for them and intervene, because we take their issues personally. However, if we advocate for only the students we care for, we miss a rich and important opportunity to open dialogue about the larger issues at hand. Perhaps this is the charge of the dialogical teacher—to open discussion of those big issues so as to lessen the need for so many micro-interventions.

From this stance, the personal connections we make with our students become braided to the academic work we do as teachers. And from those relationships comes the potential to advocate. I have come to believe it is impossible to separate the two; what is required as a dialogical teacher is the commitment to continually consider and work with the tension created by our engaged participation in these relationships.

WHAT HAVE I LEARNED ABOUT DIALOGICAL TEACHING?

If you visit my high school classroom, you'll quickly notice the walls of my room are filled with "stuff." It's all precious and important for different reasons—my Route 66 travel plate and vacation magnets speak of my love of travel and adventure beyond the classroom, the sketch of Jim Morrison that a former student drew by hand for me as a gift, my visual representation of Lucille Clifton's "Homage to My Hips" (1987) demonstrates the personal meaning I made from a favorite poem, the Rosie the Riveter ornament that reminds me I am like my own World War II warship–welding grandmother who just passed away this year.

My students' work and writing line the walls as well. The students decided the work was too good not to share and stapled them up without asking. I can't begin to describe how their sense of pride and entitlement to the space pleases me. Everything has a place of honor and usually a story behind it. It is a space that invites students to return and welcomes them to learning. Many times, new students will walk into my room and look around with wide-eyed wonder as smiles spread across their faces. I really like watching that happen, and in that moment I know I will be able to work with such students, for they've accepted my invitation to enter our classroom space, and at the very least, talk about what they find there.

Visitors often remark that my classroom doesn't look like a typical high school classroom, and I take pride in this distinction. I believe and hope they understand that the way I decorate my room is not just for the sake of the aesthetic; it reflects an environment where students claim ownership of the space because they have been invited to help create an environment where they may reveal vulnerability and take academic risks. The tokens and work samples represent this ongoing dialogue I'm having with all who enter the room. Certainly the items help put us at ease, so we may feel comfortable as we work together.

They also serve as monuments to growth and achievement. A student recently used his skills in carpentry to create a unique shelf for my classroom books. While he was a student in my class, he wasn't an exceptionally accomplished English student; however, his gift reflects his understanding that he was part of a powerful learning community and his desire to leave evidence of that achievement for future 10th-graders I've yet to meet and teach.

My hope, though, is that these items send an invitation, welcoming my students and relaying the message that I am accessible to them and open for academic conversations as well. That my classroom lets them know I'm there to help and will help is one of many ways I send a message of welcome. The fact that students like to return to my classroom on a regular basis even though I am no longer their teacher leads me to believe I have been successful at creating a home away from home for them and me.

I know what some evaluators see when they come to my classroom because they've told me; they see only a classroom of very "comfortable" students. They encourage me to nurture less and teach more, so I can only assume they see student comfort as a bad thing. In their perspective, students who are laughing and talking as they work or thoughtfully questioning their teacher couldn't possibly be doing anything rigorous enough to count as real learning.

This is where the blurred boundaries get sticky because I believe I'm doing the important work of getting them engaged and motivated enough to wade into a tough topic of discussion or into a difficult reading or writing task, or at the very least showing them how real people wrestle with complicated questions and problems. Penny Kittle (2013) said it best—"A book isn't rigorous if students aren't reading it" (p. xvi). In other words, students have to have a reason to want to try our work. Otherwise, they don't do anything and they get absolutely nothing from our teaching.

Creating opportunities for students to want to try the complex learning tasks we place before them is how I view my role in the classroom. For example, I know in my school district that argumentative writing is our end goal, but it is scary and too difficult for many of my students to attempt right out of the gate. They are not comfortable with writing, period, and this more formal writing pushes them outside their comfort zone, to say the least.

Confronted with this seemingly impossible writing task, they will refuse to do it rather than try. We must go in easy; we must slowly but surely wade into the task. To do so, I come at them with writing tasks in a form they trust. Once we are comfortable with the idea of putting words on a page and increasing the volume of their writing, then we may begin to think about pulling good quotes to back up those ideas and explaining what those quotes do to support our ideas.

They wade in with me because they are comfortable enough in the learning space to trust me not to shoot down their best first efforts, and this approach helps me later when it's time to write harder and longer and with more Common Core complexity. It isn't easy for us when we do, but it is manageable when we get there because I show them they have the tools and a way to tackle the feelings of uncertainty as they slip outside their comfort zones. The relationship that fosters comfort and trust thus strengthens our ability to attempt tasks and process learning that evoke feelings of academically rigorous and creative discomfort.

Yet my evaluators may encourage me to "push students" too far out of their comfort zones to a place of advanced academic rigor because, in the eyes of these observers, it's impossible for comfortable students to be doing anything other than easy work. I can argue that the students need to build confidence before they tackle challenging work—to dump them unprepared into tasks that are too difficult will likely lead to frustration and disengagement, and that is not a type of teaching and learning environment

I can abide. However, as the advice comes from supervisors armed with a mandate to model their interpretation and expectations of the Common Core Standards, I must navigate this relationship very carefully.

As I position myself more and more as a teacher of high school students, what I take from writing about my practice and considering my actions and classroom decisions from a dialogical stance is my belief that the relationships I build with students make learning possible. Certainly, they create a sense of comfort, and that is important because we aren't open to new and difficult things if we don't feel safe enough to try them. That sense of security also promotes a willingness to wobble with beliefs where students agree to have uncomfortable conversations for the sake of risking new learning and consider new ways of thinking.

I have learned that dialogical teaching is a stance that rewards our efforts. I can't imagine a classroom where I wouldn't engage my students with the texts and issues of their lives. I want to know about my students, and I want them to know about me. They teach me as much and as often as I teach them. This stance gives me the strength and courage to be my students' greatest advocate. I wouldn't trade this payoff for anything.

I have also learned that dialogical teaching requires great investment and heightened expectations—expectations I cannot always fulfill. Kayla's reaction to the news that I would be leaving is a prime example of this. From the outside looking in, it makes perfect sense that I want and need to challenge myself in new professional contexts. However, add in the relationships I've built through dialogical teaching and the conflict between my needs and my students' expectations, and the relationship becomes complicated.

For the dialogical teacher, the feeling of having to be fully accessible at all times is mentally and physically taxing work. I worry about burning out, but then again, I don't know how to teach any other way. It seems to me that the best way to move forward is to keep using dialogue and working with the tensions that arise, always negotiating that balance between the academic results my employer requires and the rich, meaning-making ability I know comes from building and maintaining relationships through dialogical teaching.

LISA'S SUGGESTIONS FOR ACTION

As I think about the future and extending any lessons I've learned about dialogical teaching to others, I've come to the conclusion that there is no single method for engaging in a conversation with yourself about your practice. I encourage teachers to find the tools that work, and urge them to use these tools frequently. Typically, I rely on reading and writing to help me think through issues in my classroom. I find if I devote the time to this personal dialogue, I come away with options to try. Problems seem solvable. Obstacles appear movable.

Put briefly, I suggest that other teachers try some combination of these three actions:

- Reflect on your practice by asking and answering hard questions about that practice.
- Get into the educational literature and read about what others have done.
- Take opportunities to experiment with a range of genres to write about your practice.

I can't help but return to the beginning. I opened my chapter with a memory of a summer spent in reflection. I still do this. Every summer, I commit the time and energy to what I call conversations with myself. I always start with the good and glowing. What is working well? I celebrate and congratulate myself for this success. I make plans to do this again in the coming year. I then move to the activities that did not work as I hoped or anticipated. What obstacles got in the way of progress? Is it a matter of a small change or shift on my part, or do I start over? I make plans to try again in the coming year.

What this conversation entails is truly dialogical practice in practice, for I am in dialogue with myself about my classroom, students, and my place in our social world of school.

If I could make no other suggestion for future action, I would choose to encourage teachers to engage in this vital form of self-reflection and dialogue. It does not have to be limited to an end-of-year activity. I use this practice every time I face obstacles in my classroom, whether I encounter a resistant reader who refuses to try to read for pleasure or my well-planned lesson falls flatter than flat. The self-reflective conversation I engage in when I ask myself hard questions, think, and offer up honest response has always provided me with helpful possibilities for how to proceed in the future. Do this if nothing else.

Engaging with the work of other teachers always provides outside perspectives. For example, the summer prior to implementing my new reading program, I read and researched how Donalyn Miller (2009) and Penny Kittle (2013) tackled and handled the topic of my inquiry. Doing so placed me in a position to dialogue with these authors and their texts. Their words, experiences, and advice gave me a feeling of possibility that I could do something to change my students' school experiences for the better. It also provided me with the courage to try because their work helped me see that my ideas for developing the program were situated in not just nurturing comfort but also academic-based authority. My reading of and dialogue with the text gave my own work a basis of credibility and a position from which to engage in conversation with my colleagues and administrators as I progressed.

Writing is another helpful tool in my dialogical practice. Some teachers keep journals as a method for reflection. I write poetry. Former U.S. poet laureate Billy Collins, in talking about the craft of poem making, credits commonplace irritations as the inspiration for most of his own poems. I am inspired by the quirky, comical, tense, and even frustrated words my students say in our classroom space. I write them down on a sticky note or in my writing notebook if it's handy. These words, phrases, or sentences then become the beginnings of poems. The writing helps me think deeply about the context in which they were said and what that means not only for my student-teacher relationship with that particular student but also for the future of my practice.

I have also used poetry writing as a way to make sense of tension with colleagues and administrators. For instance, when my colleague compared my style of teaching to sugar, I needed a way to think about the reference without a constant reminder of the personal hurt that this comparison conjured in my mind. So I wrote about it. I researched sugar and medicine. I wrote some more. I focused and dialed in to the important ideas at the heart of our dialogue. The writing helped me see the value in continuing the conversation with my colleague and also provided, yet again, a position from which to dialogue as an academic authority, not merely as a concerned and nurturing advocate.

For teachers wishing to engage in dialogical practice, writing is one of my top three suggestions. Writing poetry is not required. It is simply one way—my preferred method—for thinking deeply about classroom practice and the relationships that make up our world. The point is to find the type of writing that is most helpful for thinking, continuing, and extending the dialogue for future learning.

CHAPTER 4

Ian's Story

Ian Altman

Early in October 2013, my 12th-grade British literature students had an hour-long discussion about violence and the desire to have power over others. We were in the midst of reading *Macbeth*, and the previous day, the students were so bored and disengaged that I could just as well have been gnawing on my own kneecaps. This day they expected more of the same, but I thought instead we should simply talk about the play, or rather, not talk about it. I asked them, "Why do you think students fight? What drives them to start throwing their fists when they know it will be broken up in a matter of seconds, no one will 'win,' and everybody involved will get suspended? What do they believe they gain from it? Power of some kind? Why is that so important?"

My students immediately opened up. They were animated and riveted by one another's words. They talked about power relations and violence in terms of gender, tensions between African American and Hispanic students, and tension between rival gangs. They were *listening* intently to one another. One student, a young man from Mexico who works with his father as a stonemason on the weekends, talked about the perception that immigrants take jobs from citizens, but added that he only wants to make money to support his family, and said that is a kind of power too, suggesting that power is not always power over others. Other students encouraged him. Occasionally, I mentioned connections in what they were talking about to *Macbeth*, careful not to overdo it, not to make an artifice of the conversation.

Then, an administrator from the district office walked in. Discussion continued as she watched for about 5 minutes. She quietly asked a student what the Essential Question and the Common Core Standard were for the day. The student pointed to the board and said something about "developing themes." The administrator left. Before the door was shut, students burst into laughter, and one of them said through his laughter, "Mr. Altman, why the fuck they do that?" It was a beautiful moment. I had them back. The incident illustrates in a compact way the odd disproportion between conflicting views of what is important in school, between the strictures of the standards-based classroom and engaged dialogical practice.

That class is fairly representative of most classes where I work. My school is a 10-minute walk from the beautiful north campus of the University of Georgia, yet it serves one of the poorest counties in the country. To begin the demographic picture, most of our students receive free or reduced lunch, and we are a Title I district. A large majority of those students living in poverty are either African American or Latino. Most of our White students are middle class, and many of those come from families professionally concerned with education and educational structures, with parents who are teachers in the school district or professors and researchers at UGA. About 60% of our 1,500 students are African American, 20% White, and 20% Latino. There are only a handful of Asian students.

Of the Latino students, the majority are Mexican American or Mexican, although there are many, too, from Central and South American countries. Of the total student population, about 8% are undocumented. The various distinctions between national origins and documentation status affect students in ways they rarely talk about. The distinctions can also affect classroom dynamics and raise important questions about the nature, purpose, and political efficacy of teaching.

I always have such questions in mind. I was neither a literature nor an education major in college. I studied philosophy, which means, among other things, that my view of educational theories begins with questions about the nature of theory itself. I live with fundamental questions about teaching and learning as a matter of course, and they affect how I see the world. As a high school student, I was almost nonparticipatory. For the simple reason that they were assigned, I never read assigned books, and I once tried to eat an IQ test because I believed even then that all human measurement, and especially mental measurement, is inherently abusive.

I come to this work from a background in continental philosophy and comparative literature. That atypical path to teaching offers an atypical perspective on what I do. This, I believe, helps to explain what happens in my classroom in a very broad way in terms of the development of large-scale, overarching intellectual trends. I bring that perspective to my classroom and to these reflections.

There is a relevant dilemma in Western philosophy dating at least to Plato: A perfect image of an original is indistinguishable from the original; if it is distinguishable, then it is an image of something else. Hugh Kenner's small book *The Counterfeiters* (1968) plays with this problem. Kenner notes that in 1738, Vaucanson perfected a mechanical duck such that observers could wonder whether it hatched from an egg. Thus it could be asked in a new way, What exactly is the essence of this thing, *duck*?

Kenner extends these points to note that thinking machines dating from Babbage's analytical engine of 1822 through the work of Alan Turing and to tomorrow's innovations in artificial intelligence all mimic our *humanitas*, human-ness. As we all know, such machines may produce noises that correspond to groups of letters: counterfeit reading. They may produce definitions of the words: counterfeit comprehension. They may even offer and enunciate sentences to explain groupings of words defined: counterfeit interpretation and talking. Together, these constitute an image of the human experience of a text, discernible as an image but easily and often mistaken for an abstraction of the real thing.

In a way, this idea of counterfeiting resembles the case of the overworked or incompetent undergraduate who, having consulted SparkNotes, may approximate the behaviors of one who has read a book. The difference in the cases may be of kind rather than degree, but the comparison nonetheless rounds us to the decisive point, which I put as follows: Language arts standards, as currently conceived and instantiated in the Common Core, are like SparkNotes for literary learning—a putative list of behaviors that competent readers and writers ought to display. Just as a real duck might move and quack the same ways as Vaucanson's mechanical counterfeit, a competent and hardworking student may incidentally display the behaviors described in the standards. But Vaucanson's copy is not a duck, and displaying certain prescribed literate behaviors is not the same as seriously engaging and studying texts. Instead, it is a form of counterfeit schooling.

Whereas standards for mathematics, social studies, and science may specify very particular pieces of positive knowledge, English language arts standards do not. They are general and distinctly nonrelatable to specific content. On the one hand, that peculiarity gives English teachers the freedom to do nearly anything we want in the classroom and call it standards based; on the other, it makes knowledge claims based on the learning of language arts standards nearly vacuous. Differently stated, the attempt to teach in dialogical ways, and the obstacles to that attempt in a standards-based environment, together illustrate the sense in which being real with students can counteract counterfeit schooling. I use the phrase *being real* instead of something like *teaching authentically* for two reasons. First, the Heideggerian idea of authenticity has been pulverized into near meaninglessness by pop academia. Second and more importantly, *being real* is my students' terminology, and it expresses with visceral precision the need to be wary of counterfeit schooling.

To close this introduction, a word of caution: I do not consider myself a dialogical teacher in some codifiable sense. I employ dialogical methods and principles when they suit my purposes, not when they don't. My purposes themselves are in some ways inherently dialogical, and in some ways not. Unpacking the subtleties of those distinctions shall be part of the reflections that follow.

A CONFRONTATION

Immigration and the legal issues surrounding undocumented students' rights are important issues in Georgia. Georgia's Board of Regents, which sets policy for all of Georgia's public colleges and universities, passed a policy that denies undocumented students access to Georgia's top five competitive schools: Georgia Institute of Technology, the University of Georgia, Georgia State University, Georgia College and State University, and the Medical College of Georgia. Undocumented students cannot apply to those schools, and they must pay the out-of-state tuition rates for all the other public universities even if they have lived here most of their lives and graduated from high school in Georgia.

I have been deeply involved for several years in publicly advocating for those students and in finding ways for them to go to college. As a result, some local community members have called for me to be fired, a conservative commentator has written a disparaging article about me and a colleague after attending a presentation we gave on this issue at the Association of Teacher Educators conference in 2013, and I have received anonymous hate mail at school.

The issue is the politicization of the teaching profession, but in terms of this book, it is an example of the tension between the legal and the ethical. I see my work as simply acting in support of good students who deserve to go to good colleges and universities. However, because of the political context, that work, which I conduct on my own time and with my own resources, bleeds into my professional life where some see it as ethically or legally suspicious, since, to them, public school teachers are not supposed to be political advocates in the classroom. And certainly not for people they see as lawbreakers.

In the fall of 2011, a colleague and I, with support from UGA's College of Education, organized a forum at the university's student center for six of our undocumented students, three from each of our schools, to tell their stories. Our purpose was twofold: We wanted the public to hear these stories to understand what these students were going through legally, sociopolitically, and emotionally; and we also wanted to empower our students, and other students, to see that words and stories can be empowering.

At one point, during a pause in the program, a man started to debate with one of my students. My former principal, who had hired me, told me I needed to get him away from my student immediately, that he was a state senator who had supported Georgia's restrictive immigration law. The following narrative describes that event and the aftermath the following week, when the senator came to my school to be interviewed about this issue by our student news magazine staff and asked specifically to see me even though I am not the journalism teacher.

October 28: Meeting a State Senator

I walked down to the conference room in the back of our library around 3:00 today to sit in on our student news magazine staff's interview with a state senator. He had requested that I be there, presumably because I'd been so outspoken last Wednesday, October 26, at a forum featuring six undocumented immigrant students who described their plight to attendees.

At the forum the previous week, he had cornered one of my students, who tried to debate with him reasonably about the meaning of being undocumented. The senator was playing a semantic game, trying to get her to admit to being a criminal. She is fairly small; he is a tall, large man and could be an intimidating presence. She stood her ground and kept calm while he lorded over her, literally and figuratively speaking down to her. I am so proud of her in retrospect. At the time, though, I interceded and drew his fire away from her, physically moving in between them. Here was an elected official publicly trying to humiliate a 17-year-old kid—a kid whom I had taught twice and whom I care about a great deal.

The interview with the magazine staff had already begun when I arrived, but he stood and greeted me, and I said that this was the student news staff's time and that I'd just sit in the back and listen. I didn't really like being in the room with this person who'd been so rude with my student before she'd even said anything last Wednesday.

Oddly, I immediately found a way to empathize with him. He has a strange vocal tick that reminded me of my own occasional oral awkwardness: the uneven remnants of a stutter that was so bad when I was young that it was impossible for me to talk at all sometimes. One doesn't simply get over that, orally or emotionally, and so despite myself I reflexively wanted to like him.

That didn't last long. He was largely incoherent, some of his analogies made no sense, he was sometimes condescending to the student news staff members who are far more sophisticated than he realized, he was falsely conciliatory, and when he played at real logical reasoning he went in circles. I'll illustrate a couple of those points.

On his coherence and analogies: When asked whether someone is to blame for the presence of undocumented immigrants, and who that might be, he said it's like if you take a 20-dollar bill and tape it to a rock by the sidewalk, and expect to find it there the next day, but it's missing, are you to blame or is the person who took it to blame? What if the tape just came off and it blew away so that it was not clearly placed anywhere deliberately? Is the person who took it a thief, or did he just find a 20-dollar bill on the side of the road? I'm not sure what the drawn-out analogy is really about, or how it answered the question.

On being falsely conciliatory: He said he sympathizes with the plight of students who did not make the choice to come here. In the same breath, and throughout the interview, he referred to them as "illegals" and "criminals." Asked whether he would help an undocumented person who came to him asking for help obtaining legal documentation, he barely answered at all. He clearly knows the vocabulary of democracy and freedom and high ideals, but seems unwilling to deal with the ideas they signify and lacks any grasp at all of the deeper implications of recent anti-immigrant legislation.

After an hour, I stood and said that I had to go to a meeting. On the school's time and property, in the presence of students, I couldn't debate his points in an antagonistic way. He rose, too, and shook my hand again. I thanked him for coming last Wednesday and for speaking to our journalism students. He thanked me for attempting to have a civil conversation with him about this last Wednesday, and he apologized for his language and tone. I acknowledged that it had been an ugly moment and let it go. I also told him that on this issue, I couldn't care less about Democrats and Republicans and party politics, that I only want what is right for my students. He said he understood and sympathized. I imagine that he sympathized in the way an alligator might, but at least he was civil.

The tension between the legal and the ethical here consists of how the roles of citizen, teacher, and employee separate and conflate. As a teacher, I had to be wary of playing a partisan political role, at least in front of students. As an employee, I had to be wary of drawing negative attention to my school and employers, and as a citizen I felt an obligation to expose a politician's poor reasoning for what it is. As a teacher, I had to allow the journalism students to conduct their business, which they did admirably. As an employee, I had to restrain myself in order to remain employed. As a thoughtful citizen, I had to let this man know that whether he realized it or not, his attitudes toward some of my students are unreasonable and that his support for Georgia's immigration law, whether intentionally or not, is inherently racist.

I decided to remain silent for the most part during the senator's interview. As a teacher, I knew that the journalism students were handling everything very well, that the dialogue between them and the senator should remain on their terms. For their development as student journalists figuring things out in their own ways, it would have been counterproductive for me to intercede. My views were, after all, already well known.

As an employee, I did not want to deal with retaliation. Had I confronted and embarrassed him for his poor thinking and demeaning rhetoric, it is possible that I could have faced a subpoena of my school emails and a trumped-up ethics investigation. I knew I had nothing to hide and had done nothing wrong, but also that I have a higher obligation to my family and that I did not want them pulled into this.

Finally, as a citizen, I trusted that one way or another the senator would, so to speak, hang himself with his own words, and that our student journalists would help him do that. I had taught all of them before, not in journalism but in AP English language, and I trusted that they knew how badly muddled his thoughts were, how inarticulate yet dangerously fervent.

I knew that they knew this because I had taught them all about rhetorical analysis and the deep political implications of word usage. We spent time lingering over questions such as what exactly we mean when we say that a person is "American," and whether it makes logical or legal sense to say that a person is "illegal." These discussions were entirely justified in terms of the standards, and my direct role in them was always carefully disinterested and restricted mostly to Socratic questioning, with occasional clarifying suggestions.

Nonetheless, the decision to have those discussions in the first place was motivated by my politics. Does that make the decision coercive? Since it is easy to justify the discussions as rhetorical analysis in terms of the standards, no. Since most of the students knew my own political leanings on this issue because of my work outside school, despite my care not to advocate directly in school, perhaps so.

At a deeper level, that question is less relevant, and hence the relevance of the standards for rhetorical analysis falls away. My real concern was always to recognize the legitimacy and human dignity of all my students, including those who are undocumented. That is the deeper sense and the dialogical purpose in opening the question of what constitutes an "American," quite apart from my more superficial political motivations. From that perspective, I do not care whether it is wrong either to the overseers of professional ethics or to the protectors of dialogical purity. Ultimately, in the larger and more important sense, it is justified by much deeper ethical considerations of the real and concrete presence of the students themselves.

A very complicated picture of dialogical practice emerges from this situation. In some ways my actions in it are not dialogical at all. I have a particular and uncompromising view of Georgia's immigration law and the board of regents policy, that they are a new form of Jim Crow discrimination. I see them that way because they discriminate against children who have done nothing wrong. I further believe that to suggest that I should be open to the opposing view in an effort to give equal weight to both sides is disingenuous: The two sides are not of equal weight legally, ethically, or politically. That view motivates me to bring the study of immigration rhetoric into my classroom, and the justification for that in terms of the standards is merely an expedient contrivance, though it is nonetheless sufficient on professional grounds. Justifying a class discussion of the rhetoric surrounding undocumented immigrants in terms of the language arts standards becomes, not exactly false or wrong, but counterfeit.

On the other hand, what I do with that issue in the classroom is very much dialogical in some crucial ways. Perhaps it should be noted explicitly, too, that I am exceedingly careful not to criticize students for disagreeing with me, and that in my Socratic questioning, I push those who agree with me to question their premises and everything about their conclusions, so much so that they often become unsure of what they really think about the issue. I consider that to be a victory on Socratic grounds, according to the principle that wisdom begins in being aware of what one does not know.

At a deeper level, the act of prompting students to open a dialogue with this aspect of their lives and identities, and those of their undocumented peers (who are never called out as such in class), to interrogate the language we use to talk about that issue in order to help students clarify their thoughts and to make new ones, is indeed dialogical practice. In this way, the roles of teacher, employee, and citizen are discrete only in imaginary or alleged ways. Through the course of inhabiting a dialogical space, those distinctions fall away.

If that is the case, and the distinctions between the personal and professional, the political and academic, are only shadows, then, rather than imposing a false equanimity on teacher behavior, we need a different kind of ethical standard that allows for the recognition and direct consideration of students' political contexts, which are also by extension teachers' political contexts. The real or noncounterfeit justification for the discussions is in the necessity of having students ask themselves and one another who they are and what makes them worthy as human beings with real dignity, and in how issues such as immigration politics play into that. From that perspective, engaging Georgia's immigration politics and the issues facing undocumented students is a perfect example of the dialogical practice of having students engage and interrogate the texts of their own lives and their peers' lives.

A CONUNDRUM

Counterfeiting is normal for most high school English teachers. We often teach works that we love because we imagine that our enthusiasm will transfer to students. We also teach works we believe will be easily relatable to students regardless of our own tastes. In both cases, we find justification in the standards that may be legitimate, but that is also counterfeit, having little to do with our real motivations.

I teach *A Raisin in the Sun* (Hansberry, 2002) to almost all my classes because I love to help students see and grasp the importance for their own lives of Walter's transformation into a person with integrity and dignity. I do this in order to open the question of what those qualities might look like for themselves, to understand the differences between Joseph Asagai and George Murchison so that students may ask for themselves what they are doing here in this school anyway or how their attitudes toward women affect their behaviors and language, to make sense of the generational conflicts between Lena and Beneatha as a way to understand their own parents' occasional indignation, to grasp Ruth's existential despair in a way that they might apply in some way to their own yearnings.

Those dialogues have a visceral reality far more immediate and important for students than anything in the standards. The standards mention character and thematic development: something to write on the board and point to when district personnel do their 5-minute walk-throughs to check their boxes and collect their nonreal data on our "instructional practices" (i.e., teaching). Thus the standards have been met, but as an afterthought, barely worth mentioning.

One interesting and troubling tension that I encounter in teaching this play, however, is that whatever my real motivations might be, some students see it as a superficial attempt to proffer something I think will be relatable to them just because a majority of them are African American: a false mainstreaming of authentically marginalized persons. Teaching works by White males is still the default after all these years; it is seen simply as literature.

Teaching works by African American authors has an extra dimension to it, whereby the subject of being African American (or Chicano, or a woman, and so on as the case may be) becomes part of the object of study. In a way, that makes the students themselves objects of study. "Why do we always read books about Black people?" is a question I hear sometimes, as though whether I mean to or not, I become Karl Lindner from *A Raisin in the Sun*, saying, "you people." It is a tension I live with much of the time. The following narrative is the result of an experiment to change the decision to teach *A Raisin in the Sun*.

Friday Through Tuesday, January 13–17, 2012

Last year, I began my AP English language course with rhetorical analyses of the Declaration of Independence, Martin Luther King Jr.'s "Dream" (1963a) speech and his "Letter from a Birmingham Jail" (1963b), and followed these with *A Raisin in the Sun*. The thematic connections are obvious, and that is the problem. It got awfully tiring, for me and for the students. We bludgeon students with messages about equality and the evils of racism from elementary school all the way through high school. They become numb to it, bored with it, irritated by it, incredulous that we seem to think they didn't get it the first time. I don't blame them.

On the other hand, I am not willing to minimize its importance, so I've changed its focus and the way I approach it. I've kept the analyses of the Declaration of Independence and both pieces by Martin Luther King, but instead of reading *A Raisin in the Sun* after those, my students read *Of Mice and Men* concurrently, and then Chaim Potok's novel *The Chosen*. They also read more contemporary, tangentially related essays.

Things were proceeding brilliantly with the first few texts, and so we dove into *The Chosen*. Although entirely different from *Of Mice and Men* in its philosophical outlook, this novel also focuses on themes of friendship, loyalty, and the mysterious connections between people. Its two protagonists are strict Orthodox Jewish boys, Danny and Reuven, who develop a brotherly friendship. Danny is a genius with a photographic memory, but his intelligence is cold, and so his father never speaks to him except when they study Talmud. In this, he teaches his son to feel pain, and hence to see it in others.

Midway through our study of this book, on a Friday afternoon after class, five students lingered in my classroom giggling over something. They were three girls and two boys, all very bright kids. I overheard one of them say, "He looks Arab," and another respond, "No, he looks Jewish." I asked what they were giggling about, and one of them happily handed me a picture they had drawn, a caricature of one of the two boys making him look stereotypically Jewish, with a huge nose, big unkempt curly hair, protruding lips, and a big head on a small body. It looked like something out of *Der Stürmer* [a weekly Nazi tabloid], circa 1938.

Some wellspring of feeling I had long since forgotten erupted in me, irrational and visceral. It was an indescribable hurt that made me feel my Jewishness in that low, brick in the bottom of the soul way that I hadn't really felt since middle school when I got into a fight with a 16-year-old 8th-grader who fancied himself a neo-Nazi skinhead: a pure, absolute, heavy, grief-laden, glass-walled alienation. As they looked at me expectantly, I put myself in order.

I handed the picture back to the students and said to them all, "Where are your heads?" Their faces changed, and their mouths hung slightly open. They stared at me part vacantly and part bewildered. One weakly said, "It's just a joke." I replied, "Yes. Where are your heads?" Not knowing what to say, they left awkwardly and dismayed, not really sure what my question meant, unsure whether I was angry at them. I, too, was unsure. I wanted them to chew on it and figure it out for themselves as I needed to.

I felt low, but stupidly low, realizing that somehow I had allowed this foolishness to strip away decades of maturation and what I had thought was rhinoceros-thick skin.

After about 10 minutes, three of the students came back. They tentatively walked in, and one of them asked if I was busy. They all had tears on their faces. I knew what was coming, and felt sympathy for them. What they were trying to do was obviously difficult, but I thought it best not to prompt them, to let them wrestle with it so that it would come out as honestly as it could. They each said how sorry they were, how embarrassed they were, how bad they felt. I thanked them for coming back, said I knew it was difficult for them, that I know they are good kids and that I believe their apologies are sincere, and asked them to sit down for a few minutes. It seemed like a good moment to make some connections with them, but I was unsure of how to proceed. This is not something one plans for, and I am a muller, often slow to think on my feet.

Without forethought, I handed them an article I had written about helping my undocumented students, and asked them to take a few minutes to read it. I had decided it was important at that moment to directly reinforce the connection of democratic values and virtues to individual care for other persons. Prior to this point, though, I had not mentioned to the class that I am Jewish, and hadn't intended to at this moment. It seemed almost cruel, and beside the point. I had forgotten that the article has these lines towards the end: "As man, teacher, father, Jew, Georgian, American, human being, and as their friend, [I] am morally diminished when the state in which I've made my home, from which I draw my salary, refuses, out of the sheerest ignorance and meanness, to allow these kids to live their lives like the rest of us" (Altman, 2011).

After I remembered what is in those lines, I began hoping they would still think of this as a lesson specific to all individual persons. The three students finished reading the article, sat back, and looked up at me. They were mortified, and had no idea what to say. They each quietly stammered again how sorry they were. I told them that I didn't wish to belabor the point, but that I hoped they now realized what the purpose was of everything we've been doing this semester. They nodded and said yes, and apologized again. The following Monday was the Martin Luther King Jr. holiday.

We finished studying *The Chosen* that Friday, and they were deeply affected by it, not, I hope, by the "Jewishness" of the book, but by the power of the relationships between Danny and Reuven and between those characters and their fathers.

To me, this episode illustrates one of the slipperiest problems with language arts standards. To anticipate briefly, almost anything we do with a text may be called standards based. The problem in this case is not so much that they are limiting but that they are empty, and not really standards at all, and hence, counterfeit. Much of the excitation around the Common Core language arts standards, both positive and negative, amounts to a rhetorical Potemkin village. Students can master the standards very well and not have learned anything of real importance.

That is what happened in the episode with *The Chosen*. This seemingly odd claim makes sense when we analyze a couple of real classroom situations, beginning with this question: What do we really want students to learn from the texts we choose for them? For me, it makes very little sense to say that we want them to learn the standards. One standard says, "Determine two or more themes or central ideas of a text and analyze their development over the course of the text, including how they interact and build on one another to produce a complex account; provide an objective summary of the text." Another says, "Demonstrate knowledge of eighteenth-, nineteenth-, and twentieth-century foundational works of American literature, including how two or more texts from the same period treat similar themes or topics." So, we may compare *A Raisin in the Sun* to *The Crucible* (Miller, 2000) and analyze the development of the themes of guilt and integrity in both. But that means we are analyzing those two themes in those two plays, and not two other themes in two other plays. Furthermore, what students in my class may learn about the plays may be radically different from what students in other classes learn about them even if they all study the same texts. In what exact sense, then, may we call their learning standards based?

A student may understand Walter Younger's integrity in *A Raisin in the Sun* but not John Proctor's in *The Crucible*. We cannot then say whether that student has mastered either standard. If we treat each play as half of the "content" of this adumbration of these two standards, perhaps the student has mastered 50% of one standard, or the other, or both. But what would that percentage signify? It would seem merely to be a metaphor for that quality of understanding by which Walter Younger's standing up to Karl Lindner to establish his family's honor can be made sense of whereas John Proctor's choosing to die to preserve his sense of honor cannot. But that means it is not a measurement, it is unfit to be graphed, and it is not really a datum from which we may discern any further fact. Furthermore, the "objective summary of [a] text" demanded by the standard is one for which a student must choose what details to include and to exclude, rendering it subjective.

These are not just dilemmas, but internal contradictions, meaning that to have learned these standards is the same as not to have learned them. Hence these standards, in and of themselves, do not actually express anything. They are in that sense nonreal, counterfeit, *unless* the actual object of study is a literary text after all, in which case texts are not mere doorways to standards but real objects of study. Because of the contradictions internal to standardized literary learning, those standards are not standards.

Must a teacher in this world of learning be fake? Rather than teachers play that game, it is much more fruitful for students' development to open broadly a dialogue about Walter Younger and John Proctor's character transformations and what integrity might have to do with that. As soon as we do that, however, we are talking about books and ideas rather than standards and "themes." In this case, the very emptiness of the standards nonetheless has a kind of substance that gets in the way of the real, productive learning that happens through dialogical practice.

Consider a different example with a different standard, concerning the understanding of setting. The standard says, "Analyze the impact of the author's choices regarding how to develop and relate elements of a story or drama (e.g., where a story is set, how the action is ordered, how the characters are introduced and developed)." Scott Fitzgerald (*The Great Gatsby*, 1925) says:

> Their house was even more elaborate than I expected, a cheerful red and white Georgian Colonial mansion overlooking the bay. The lawn started at the beach and ran toward the front door for a quarter of a mile, jumping over sun-dials and brick walks and burning gardens—finally when it reached the house drifting up the side in bright vines as though from the momentum of its run. The front was broken by a line of French windows, glowing now with reflected gold, and wide open to the warm windy afternoon, and Tom Buchanan in riding clothes was standing with his legs apart on the front porch. (p. 11)

Whether we take the school-conventional view that Fitzgerald is following the novel-conventional process of offering a setting for a character before introducing him, or Kenner's (1975) deeper and more interesting view that the description of the property is not "setting" but a list of things purchased from which we are to discern Tom Buchanan's values, we may fairly be said to be addressing that standard. But already we can see the emptiness in that assertion, since if we may teach that the passage means two very different things, and both may fulfill the same requirement, then the requirement, or standard, has no content, almost as though it is not there.

The genuinely dialogical approach to such a passage would be to let students make of it what they will, to transact with it on their own terms and make their own meaning, or perhaps to offer the two roughly defined possibilities and encourage them to debate it while not forcing the issue one way or the other. If we follow that procedure, we end up in the same conundrum:

We cannot say whether we have addressed the standard or not because the standard tells us nothing but that students must analyze the impact of the author's choices. If it is truly as open ended as it sounds, then we can safely ignore it and still claim to have taught it, which makes little sense.

If some content is meant to be implied, if it in fact, however weakly, directs us to some particular *kind* of interpretation, which may presumably (and also weakly) be tested (A, B, C, or D), then the teacher is immediately thrown into two conflicts. First, he or she must object that the standard is so poorly conceived and written that any specific content it may prescribe is not actually discernible. (And of course we do object in that way, but no one is listening. Or we are told to "deconstruct" the standard, a meaningless directive that comes from an absurd misapprehension of postmodern philosophical language.) Second and more pertinent, the teacher must choose whether to risk letting students make of Fitzgerald's prose what they will, to dialogue and transact with it and make their own meanings, and risk not "getting" whatever it is to which the standard is presumed to direct them.

So we come again to the question of what we want students to learn from texts. What if I had let those five students go on with their racist caricature without forcing them to think about its cruelty? Could they be said to have understood the work we had done to that point in the semester? In that moment between bottling my personal, emotional reaction to the caricature and deciding to have them read my article, I realized that they had not really considered the political implications of having individual, human empathy.

There is no question that they could have written great essays about all the literature we studied and sustained interesting class discussions. They knew the right words to say, and a standards-based grading rubric would no doubt have rendered high marks. Yet it would all have been counterfeit, falsehoods built on expectations both implicit and explicit that tell students which ideas to parrot and in what forms.

It may seem that the design of the curriculum had the objective of forcing students to have a certain view of human rights, democratic social values, and empathy for others. That interpretation of the situation is valid, and it seems to describe a nondialogical approach to literary learning. On the other hand, without that approach, without the directed agenda, not as a specific set of necessary normative ethical beliefs but simply as an orienting framework, a set of issues within which we have dialogue, it is hard to imagine what purchase a dialogical approach could have with students. To engage in a dialogue with the texts of their lives requires that students become aware of what questions there are to ask, and that leads inevitably into questions of social justice. In the specific contexts of the South and of my school, that means opening questions, sometimes uncomfortably, of race, poverty, immigration, and religious discrimination.

However we may wish to judge these situations, it should be clear that the Common Core Standards, which I am directed to teach, have almost no bearing at all on what I do, and yet my students learn a great deal, and develop good skills anyway, which means that whether I mean to or not, I do teach the standards. The Common Core Standards for English Language Arts, then, as a kind of overlay, impose a *reductio ad absurdum* on what we do, but only if we claim to take them seriously and believe they have some discernible intellectual substance.

BEING REAL AND WRITING IT

Counterfeiting extends to teaching writing. So, to close by way of return to the initial episode of this chapter, I introduce a distinction between writing and school writing. We often treat the teaching of writing as a kind of athletic contest, with time limits and minimum boundaries and maximum boundaries, often on topics profoundly unrelatable to students' real lives. One former Georgia High School Writing Test prompt told students to "write a speech to . . . convince . . . senior citizens that they should give their services to benefit the community." Many of my students' grandparents and great-grandparents still work minimum wage jobs to keep the rent paid and the lights on.

When we do ask students to write in ways that may have real significance for their lives, the standards-based emphasis is on form, structure, rhetoric, syntax, diction, precise phrasing: the *skills* of writing. Those are not unimportant, but they do not by themselves constitute good writing.

Several years ago, as a new department chair, I was tasked with improving my school's graduation writing test scores, as they had declined sharply over previous years. We developed a plan to increase the passing rate that involved identifying those students likely not to pass, pulling them from their elective classes, and tutoring them intensively during our planning periods. Each period had about 30 students and 2 to 4 English teachers. Everyone in the department gave up planning periods to do this for 7 school days. We called it the writing "blitz," which was horrifying but appropriate, as we were indeed attacking these students with standardized writing practice.

We taught them to analyze the prompts, to "find" the topic, "find" the audience, "find" their purpose for writing, as though they were finding the slope in $y = mx + b$. We taught them to decide what their opinions are on the issue in each practice prompt and brainstorm reasons to support their opinions. We never mentioned that one might not have an opinion until one writes about an issue; that simply arguing for or against something usually does not reflect much thinking; that having to invent an argument for a position might mean it's a weak position; that writing is also a dialogue with oneself, and with other people. Such considerations would not have helped them pass the test, would probably have caused some to fail it. This kind of work is what I call *instruction*, as opposed to teaching. Instruction is what one reads in a manual: how to install new brake pads or manipulate a graphing calculator.

Our instructions worked. Our students did well on the test, better than ever before, and did again the following year: the expected result of thoroughly nondialogical teaching. That does not mean the students we tutored knew how to write well or that they understood the importance of writing. Certainly most had no sense of the joy to be found in writing, the joy of having a dialogue with one's own ideas laid bare on the paper, and through that dialogue understanding new thoughts one did not know one had in oneself. Why should they, when all the writing they have done is for school and involved topics with which they are not concerned and grading that they fear because it only tells them what they have done wrong?

Or, for the well-read and well-skilled students, grading that tells them they are great writers but that often indicates that the teacher, knowing the students' good skills, only skimmed the work, making the whole exercise perfunctory and counterfeit: doing school as though doing a tornado drill. This includes the artifice of time limits that produce forced reasoning, harried style, and a glut of other problems. Teaching writing according to the standards thus normalizes the extreme extroversion of our culture—say it quickly and loudly, in a way everyone will understand without having to work too hard, or you won't be heard at all.

Consider a dialogical writing space in contrast: the forum we held in 2011 for undocumented students and the work my three students put into the narratives they produced, narratives that floored the majority of the audience with admiration and respect. The students were the experts on their own lives; the occasion gave them the impetus to reach into themselves to tell of themselves; the topic was one of importance not only for them but for everyone listening; they were able to say for themselves, on their own terms and in their own ways, who they are and why they deserve to be taken seriously as human beings. *That* was important, and real, and that situation was inherently dialogical: They were telling an audience of their humanity, and the audience, including the belligerent senator, responded.

My teaching, in that case, was dialogical facilitating. I asked them a few questions and discussed their answers with them, which prompted them to think and draw their own stories out of themselves. Notably, the first question I asked each of them was, "Do you feel comfortable doing this and is it important enough to you to 'come out' like this?" Only after they assented did I ask, "What about this situation is most important to you—emotionally, legally, and pragmatically? How can you make this into a story that will matter to those listening? How do you think I can best help you do that?" It was true dialogue, including the awareness to leave them alone in silence. It was not the rhetorical pole vault that, however participatory with students, is really only my performance. It was easily the best and most important teaching I did that year although I "did" very little. I only wish I had been able to do it in my official position as a teacher.

What unifies all these experiences in this chapter are the various types of conflict between the real and the counterfeit, that is, between learning that has as its object things about which we can make legitimate claims, and learning that has no discernible object or merely putative objects. The former may result in some claims of knowledge, the latter in what I call *counterfeit knowledge*. The cause of the counterfeit is the standardization of literary learning that only seems to have some content, though it is in fact empty. Since many curricular decisions, including contradictory ones, may fill it, it makes no sense to call language arts standards *standards*. The way to give some sense and seriousness to the whole ludicrous endeavor is to make students themselves into texts and extensions of texts, however discomfiting that may sometimes be to everyone concerned. In other words, students, as dialogical subjects, *are* a resistance to counterfeit schooling.

Ian's Suggestions for Action

Engaging controversial ideas in school is always risky. Each context determines its particular set of risks. There is no plan or formula that will eliminate risk. You must simply understand your context and decide in full awareness how much and what kinds of risks to take. Here are some guidelines that may help assuming risk effectively:

- Understand your context; know your building and district administration and fellow teachers, your students, their parents, and the community.
- Frame all disputes carefully in terms of helping students.
- Develop trusting and professionally respectable relationships with all concerned.
- Accept and encourage dissenting views and arguments, and make that fun. (Self-deprecating humor helps.)
- Take the same risks in your writing that you ask of students.

Risking Public Standing

Once a teacher has decided take a risk, she should embrace it, and always be ready to justify it appropriately. For example, advocating for undocumented students in Georgia, against the views of my own state senator, has earned me criticism, and even hate mail. When questioned, I always frame the discussion in terms of the interests of students I am charged with teaching. Thus I can claim without prevarication that it makes no difference to me who is a Republican or a Democrat, that my only concern is for my students, and if that pits me against the Republican party in Georgia, so much the worse for me. I accept the risk I have taken, but in doing so, earn the respect of students, parents, colleagues, administrators, and the majority of the Athens community.

Risking Classroom Equanimity

Similarly, when a teacher is publicly known to hold certain views that are politically charged, there is no point in disowning them or affecting a false equanimity in the classroom. That would be disingenuous, and most students know better. The only way to deal with it is to be open to challenge and to encourage challenges, to honor students who forcefully take up those challenges, and indeed to make strong arguments against one's own known beliefs. That is not especially difficult, and indeed it can be fun. Students always seem to appreciate the show of vulnerability.

I recently published an article criticizing the state legislature's demand that the AP U.S. history course be what they consider more conservative and patriotic. A state senator then published a defense of the legislature. I gave my students both articles and instructed them to choose the one they agree with more, and argue against it. I did the exercise with them, taking up the senator's cause against my own piece, and had a great time doing so.

Risking the Self

It is important also in writing to demonstrate the risks one asks students to take. I always assign a narrative identity essay, which asks students to tell stories that illustrate who they are, whatever facets of themselves they think most pertinent, and how that transacts with the identity that others or the world at large see upon them. They present these to their classmates. I do this assignment too and present it, telling them that it is not fair to ask them to put themselves out there unless I am willing to go with them. I also present mine in the middle of the pack, never at the beginning or the end, because I do not wish to set some standard they feel they must measure up to and do not wish to make the exercise about me.

In each of these three cases, the point, or tactic, is to illustrate what it looks like to live with the risks one takes in occupying one's chosen place in the world. That is the closest thing to practical advice I can offer: Own your actions and views, but do so in a way that is helpful to all your students.

CHAPTER 5

Angela's Story

Angela Battaglia Dean

For many of us who teach, preplanning is that brief period of time in late summer before school hallways flood with students and when teachers are supposed to be planning lessons and readying rooms for the upcoming weeks. In actuality, most of preplanning is spent in mandated meetings. Still, during one such time, I managed to find an open period in which to roam the relatively quiet halls of my high school and peek into the rooms of some of my colleagues.

As I wandered, I noticed that several teachers had posted what were supposed to be inspirational posters on the wall next to their doors. I'm sure you've seen similar ones; they often feature a drenched cat or majestic eagle, the "You can do it!" sort of posters. I also noticed similar posters hung next to the clock or by the pencil sharpener inside the classrooms. Based on the obvious placement outside and around the interior of the room, it was clear that these posters were meant to be seen every day by students.

Some of the posters were commenting on bad attitudes. One specifically read, "The attitude STOPS here!" As I passed this poster, I wondered how the kids would feel about being met with such a message before they've even met this person on the other side of the door. Though each student will not enter the room with the assumed chip on their shoulder, each student is met with this message regardless. I wondered if the assumption, so clearly stated to them as they entered, would lead to only developing negative tension in the classroom, and thus create the attitude the poster owner so wanted to avoid.

While such posters are hung at the beginning of each year with good intentions, they can be seen as, depending on the student and the day, demands rather than requests. Such messages posit the student in a powerless position and situate the teacher, whom the students may not have even met yet, as a voice of authority. A tension is already created before teacher and class have even uttered a word to each other.

Unfortunately, assumptions about students did not end with passive messages posted outside and inside teachers' classrooms. Once school was in session, at the end of each day the student resource officer (SRO) came on the intercom and shouted, "All students not under the direct supervision of a teacher or coach must exit the building immediately!" It was usually repeated several times in a threatening way. He would come back on 15 or 20 minutes later and say it again. I wondered, when we heard the repeated message, a bit louder and a bit more forceful, if the SRO had just caught more kids loitering in the halls and felt vindicated by making his announcement again.

Previously, the community school secretary would make the announcement, but perhaps her voice was too kind and the kids didn't scramble out of the building like they did to the out-of-breath, barking voice that replaced it. It also used to be that they had a good 30 minutes or more before the announcement was made, but that changed to the SRO's coming on directly after the dismissal bell rang. I sometimes wondered if kids broke into a cold sweat at their lockers trying to get out of the hall before the SRO could catch them at 2:25.

It was here that I began to consider the dialogue of school, and whether posters and intercom messages directly influence the dialogues of teachers, students, and staff. Reflecting on the SRO's announcement, how it echoed off the walls of the school, made me angry. Mostly because this was not a dialogue at all. Much as with the posters in my colleagues' classrooms, students could not actively engage in a response to the SRO's commands. In fact, I knew that once they were delivered, the students were hunted down and barked at again for not complying. There were no exchanges between the SRO and students so that understanding might be found. Rather, the SRO grew indignant that they had not heeded his dictates.

I believe the school belongs just as much to the students as it does to the adults, if not more. I understand the importance of supervision and looking out for the well-being of students, but the way in which this message was delivered and acted upon troubled me. The authoritarian and antagonistic role of the SRO parallels the adult figures we see portrayed in John Hughes's films of the 1980s. Like Vice Principal Vernon of the *Breakfast Club* (Tanen, Hughes, & Hughes, 1985) and Principal Rooney of *Ferris Bueller's Day Off* (Hughes, Jacobson, & Hughes, 1986), the SRO refused to take any crap from the students he encountered and assumed the worst about all students he came into contact with in the hallways.

The difference is that in Hughes's films the kids have the upper hand and are victorious over those who work to control them. Rebellion for our students would be risky and might have severe consequences. In the eyes of the school's SRO, for a student to merely try to explain that she is going to her locker to get a forgotten textbook after a practice or a club meeting would be a sign of defiance. She should simply stay quiet and comply with his demands. My concern is how this posits all adults in the building as authoritarian and antagonistic. It encourages the assumption that all students are up to no good and need to be controlled, and perhaps fosters the stereotypical adult-child relationships we see highlighted in Hughes's films.

This daily harangue worked as a constant reminder to students of their position in the school and adults' lack of interest in their needs and their reasoning for their actions. The tone and word choice did and always will anger me because I do not want to be identified with the message or the messenger. It angers me because I see the ways this 2-second message can hinder those of us who want to engage in dialogue with our students in our classrooms. Much like the poster about attitudes, this message can shut down students before they even enter my door. My observations of how the school "spoke" to the students made me realize that the talk was filled with assumptions and accusations, and it positioned students as powerless in that they had no voice. These conversations were noxious or directly confrontational, but the student was expected to simply comply.

These instances led me to wonder about the dialogue of school. I don't mean just the conversations we have in class with students. I wonder about the verbal and written messages we all hear and read each day in the school building. I wonder about the lasting effects this one-sided imparting of messages has on students and faculty members. How it affects our relationships with one another. How it positions each of us in an "us versus them" game of submission and control. Who "us" or "them" might be shifts according to who the message's intended audience might be. Though the receiver of this message may not be able to converse with the message's creator, a tension is developed. Receivers of the message interpret it according to their past experiences and respond in relation to those past experiences. One cannot converse with a poster or a squawking intercom, but the tensions such messages develop around relationships between student and the faculty or the faculty and the administration shape future interactions.

The aim of this chapter is to demonstrate some of the ways we can move away from the squawking-box classroom and, instead, develop and foster a dialogical classroom. The chapter, however, will also explore some of the impediments to doing so with students who have been conditioned to exist within a space that does not necessarily value the voice that the dialogical classroom strives to elicit from each individual in the classroom. I focus this chapter on how I attempted to create a dialogical classroom over the course of a year. My intention is to illustrate the ways in which dialogue can be created and destroyed in a 10th-grade English language arts classroom using various texts and discussion protocols to foster a dialogical classroom. Much as in the opening observations, I also focus on a discussion around positions of power and difficult choices the dialogical classroom presents for the teacher. I also consider the constraints—either the daily schedule or the demographics of the classroom—that can contribute to tensions.

DESCRIBING THE CONTEXT

I worked in a large and diverse suburban school just northeast of a large southern city. The area of the county in which I worked had a mixture of upscale subdivisions and multifamily housing, consisting of either town-homes or apartment buildings. The student population was representative of America's demographic makeup, with approximately 43% of the population being European American, 15% African American, 15% Hispanic, 12% Asian, 5% of mixed racial/ethnic background, and 10% unreported. Most students had been born in other parts of the country and had relocated to the area for the prospect of lower costs of living. At the time of the study, approximately 30% of the student population received free and reduced lunch.

A school filled with 3,700 students and 300 faculty and staff members will certainly create tension-filled dialogues, so no doubt the setting made me sensitive to monologic exchanges. Because relaying messages to large groups of people can be done easily through intercom announcements and posters, it makes sense that the school used these methods. Unfortunately, doing so also allows for the message to be conveyed without having to hear a response, positive or negative.

Through these means of mass communication, our students are shown again and again that we truly do not want to engage with them, that they should just listen and comply. At one point, I watched as two young men were chastised in the cafeteria for the way they were dressed. I heard one cafeteria staff member say to these two African American boys, "Even the special ed kids know how to keep their pants pulled up. Why can't you?" If they had attempted to defend themselves or even defend the special education students who also had been denigrated, they would have been seen as troublemakers. All they could do was tug at their waistbands and shrug the experience off.

Equally troubling was my silence. I was in shock from what I had witnessed, but beyond that, I felt I could not step in to defend the boys because it would undermine the cafeteria staff member. I was caught outside my classroom—where engaged dialogical practice was the norm—and fell into line with the expectation of the monologue of the school where authoritarian messages are given without room for retort.

This is one of the challenges for one who does engage in dialogical classrooms in a school that does not. In your dialogical classroom, students can find their voice and express it. But then, what happens to those students when they leave the classroom with that voice? Or what happens to the teacher who uses her voice in a school or a system that may not want to hear it?

I do not understand how this antagonistic relationship has developed and why sharing ideas or even talking through ideas is seen as threatening. As educators, many of us are angry, but our responses sometimes come across much as the angst of teenagers explored in those John Hughes films. We complain among ourselves and rage against the policies, but too many of us are too terrified to actually act or insert our voice, and thus we empower those who are working to dismantle our profession. Sadly, it was not surprising to see this angst acted out in the faculty copy room of my school. I reflected:

The messages we get as teachers in the copy room have come to really weigh me down. Someone has posted the steps the state is taking with the new evaluation system. This came out last year (2011), and it is presented as 14 frequently asked questions (FAQs) and bulleted points to answer these questions. Someone has written below, "14 reasons to retire early." Not far away hangs a political cartoon. In it the teacher is passing back papers and a student has his in his hand. The grade on the paper reads, "F" and the student has a dialogue bubble above his head. He asks the teacher whether she can risk giving out such bad grades since her pay is now tied to student success. He says something smart like he'd hate to see her lose her job or make less money.

Each of these examples shows the monologic nature of relationships within my school. My fear is that we have grown all too accustomed to the one-sided messages we post, give, and receive in our schools. My fear is the effect that such a relationship has on the transactions among faculty, staff, and students. What tensions might achieve more equilibrium if there were opportunities for all to enter into a dialogical relationship? Certainly, working to understand one another would reveal new tensions, but the hope is that through those tensions, addressed through dialogue, understanding can be achieved. Dialogue, however, has to be a two-way street.

I teach in a dialogical way because I feel that my voice cannot be the only one in the classroom. I am uncomfortable with the imposed monologic nature of the discourses of school. We, my students and I, must muddle through making meaning of texts in relation to our lives and the world around us so as to have a greater understanding of who we are and to feel that we are agents within our world. In *The Pedagogy of the Oppressed*, Paulo Freire (1970) writes,

Through dialogue, the teacher-of-the-students and the students-of-the-teacher cease to exist and a new term emerges: teacher-students with students-teacher. The teacher is no longer merely the one-who-teaches, but one who is himself taught in dialogue with the students, who in turn while being taught also teach. They become jointly responsible for a process in which all grow. (p. 80)

When I walk the halls and observe how teachers speak to students or watch the news and hear how policymakers speak about and to teachers, I become frustrated. No one can grow in the current environment, and if anything, the message I feel we are passing along to students and teachers is that we do not really want them to grow, but to quietly comply.

LEANING TOWARD DIALOGICAL PRACTICE

I focus this chapter on one of my college preparatory 10th-grade classes. The school had three tracks for students. College preparatory was considered by many in the school to be the "lowest" track, but could be filled with a mix of abilities and levels of engagement. A student who is in the gifted program, but who behaves in apathetic ways toward school, might sit next to a student who reads at a 6th-grade level. The assumption of the district is that all students will be prepared to go to college upon graduation from high school. The minority groups in the school are also overrepresented in the college preparatory classes, which are largely made up of African American and Hispanic students and predominately males. White and female students find themselves in the minority in the college preparatory classroom.

For my 10th-graders, I develop our yearlong study of world literature around a single question: What does it means to be a citizen of the world? I feel that through the thematic connections of the texts, students will see a connection to themselves. We work our way through the ancient civilizations and into modern day, returning to the question again and again. While the anchor text may be from an ancient civilization, I try to pair it with various texts that get at similar themes and issues. The pairings of ancient with modern, I hope, helps my students to see connections between themselves and a text like *The Epic of Gilgamesh* (Sandars, 1972) or an excerpt from the *Mahabharata* (Anonymous & Smith, 2009). In this way, we spend a year together in dialogue with one another and with the texts we read.

Unpacking a Wobble Moment

One day early in our year together, I brought in an excerpt from Sandra Cisneros's *The House on Mango Street* (1991). Specifically, it was the chapter titled "Those Who Don't." Below is an excerpt from my narrative on how I hoped the student would see how this text and others we discussed in class "talked" to one another in dialogue and thus provide us with a way to dialogue with one another. The day, however, did not go by without tension.

Oh, trying to get the dialogue going . . .

I have my 4th period divided up in groups and sitting in fours and threes around the room. We've been reading and writing about the question and how it applies to the various texts we've explored for the majority of the beginning weeks of school. I've started with Chimamanda Adichie's TED talk, "The Danger of a Single Story" and ended with JR's TED talk on how art can change the world. It is a Friday and we will play MLK [high school in football] away tonight.

We had a terrific discussion the day prior on JR's speech. The kids engaged with one another, came to a consensus on their ideas about the speech, and then shifted smoothly into a whole-class discussion like they'd been doing this with me for weeks. This had actually been our first attempt at group discussion. I had a student sitting on the top of the back of his seat, trying to get as in on the whole-class discussion as he physically could. Those who typically might sit silently and let others speak for them offered up their ideas. As the end of class came, the excitement of our discussion and what we'd just generated permeated the room and left smiles on most of our faces. I made sure to tell them how awesome they'd done and how well the discussion had gone.

Then came Friday. It just happened to be the very next day. Same groups. Same desks. Same kids. Different energy. I've got several who look as though they are ready to shut down and go back to bed. Two girls are arguing over something that has nothing to do with the text. The boy in the group ducked his head to stay clear of their dispute. I kept coming over to provide proximity control only to find that I was distracting the other group sitting by the bickering girls. I tried to refocus them all and moved away.

They were supposed to be examining a portion of *The House on Mango Street* called "Those Who Don't." Because the shifting of the text can sometimes be difficult, I asked students to consider some guided-reading questions. Our somewhat functional groups seemed to wonder what race the people in the text were. The guided question that led them there, I think, said something to the effect of "Whom is the narrator speaking about in the first paragraph?" Then the lines "all brown all around, we are safe" were referenced as evidence for their interpretations. I knew this would be the question at the heart of our discussion, so we shifted to a whole-class discussion.

We jumped into the question of race and the kids all had their reasons for thinking that the narrator was Black or Hispanic. Then I asked if the race of the narrator really mattered and asked them to look at the last line of the text, "That's how it goes and goes." We discussed what they thought that meant and whether it was true. So far the whole-class discussion was going well. Someone suggested that perhaps the narrator was a hypocrite, since she seemed to criticize those who came into the neighborhood and passed judgment, but then she did the same passing of judgment in other neighborhoods. This is when my senior who is repeating the course and another White student at his group began to voice their opinions.

They seemed to feel that it was common sense when you go into a bad or dangerous neighborhood that you take certain precautions. Jeffery explained that he would put his wallet in his front pocket when he headed down to the game tonight against MLK. Jeffery is one of four White students in this class. I understood his intentions with this comment were perhaps harmless because I understood his perspective was shaped by the context in which he lived as a White young man from the suburbs; in his way of thinking, he was being cautious.

His explanation, however, didn't go over well with the rest of the group. No one really verbalized their discontent with what he was suggesting about Blacks and Hispanics in the inner city, and perhaps unintentionally about his Black and Hispanic classmates, but the feeling in the room shifted and conversations went to the tables or shut down all together.

As the White teacher, if I defend his statements or say anything that may sound like I'm aligning with his comments, I'll lose the rest of them. If I allow for a statement to be made and just let it hang there in the room, how will further discussions on sensitive topics go? If I allowed for the kids to press him on what he meant, how will that build community? If I press him, how will he feel entering the room again tomorrow? I don't recall what I said exactly, but I know I left with a feeling that I hadn't said what I could or what I wanted.

This incident illustrates how easily the dynamics of a classroom can shift from day to day and moment to moment. We had been moving right along and seemingly in concert with one another while we discussed the two TED talks, but when we moved to the excerpt from *The House on Mango Street* we had what my middle school band director would call a "train wreck." The impending crash was not easy for me to foresee, even with the two bickering girls in one group. I assumed we could move seamlessly into a whole-group discussion around the text, but that was exactly when things fell apart.

This is the challenge of the dialogical classroom. Students explore their voices, and in a diverse classroom, their voices are not always going to align with their classmates. It is easy for the teacher to jump in and take over the conversation and make the students sit and listen. At the beginning of the year when students are formulating an opinion of how the classroom will operate and what kind of teacher you are, as a dialogical teacher it is dangerous to shift into that mode even if it may be easier. By doing so, I run the risk of perpetuating a system where the students are silenced, or perhaps worse yet, a system where they learn that in order to appeal to me, they just need to wait for me to state what I want them to say and then restate it to pass the class.

So I asked myself, was it that the students were butting up against the text, or the discussion? I attempt to connect their personal lives to the texts we read, helping them to see the personal in the academic so that the academic does not seem so abstract or cold or ancient. For the most part, students are engaged and discussing the assignment in their small groups. My desire to shift that to a whole-class discussion is where things become a bit more difficult and even tension filled.

When a different kind of dialogue intrudes or interrupts the dialogue that had taken place in small groups, tensions are created. It would seem that shifting toward a large-group discussion would be a natural movement in the dialogical classroom, but clearly on this particular day and setting they seem to conflict with one another. Within their individual groups, dialogue was successful, but when Jeffery shared with the whole class his interpretation of the text, classroom dialogue got more complex than perhaps the class and I were ready to handle.

Jeffery did what the assignment and what I had asked of him. He had related to the text in a personal way, even if his relating to the text positioned him as no different from the narrator whom the class had negatively labeled a hypocrite for calling out strangers passing judgment on her neighbors, but then passing similar judgment when she finds herself in a strange neighborhood. His understanding of why one might take certain precautions when going into a neighborhood different from one's own, or for him the football game later that night in an unfamiliar part of a major city, seemed to be defended by the text. For Jeffery, it was common sense to have a distrust of those you do not know or who do not appear to be like you or those you know.

We did not get the opportunity to consider his stance through self-examination. Since I did not feel that I had established enough of a foundation with this group at this point in the year, I feared pushing his statement further or challenging him. I had asked for volunteers and he answered my call; to turn the conversation into a possible attack on what he shared would have potentially shut Jeffery down for the remainder of the year.

I believe this decision highlights one of the concerns in a dialogical classroom. We have to wonder how much our identity as teacher, a position of power, sways dialogue, especially in difficult situations like the one this narrative illustrates. Much like Ian and his questioning of his pushing of the four students after school over the caricature, I found myself in a difficult position. I wanted to continue more in my role as a facilitator, but feared that whatever I might have said would have only guided them to one resolution, and I was not happy about any possible resolution. I did not want to have Jeffery made out to be the outsider while the rest of us sat in judgment of his stance. I did not want to ignore his contribution to our discussion. Though it may have been off-putting to many, he was engaging in a dialogical way by bringing his experiences and ways of reading the world into his interpretation of the text. He was doing what I had asked.

It being Friday and our only having 55 minutes to work together, I had to leave the discussion where it was and hope that the weekend would put some space between us and what had taken place. I also hoped that the weekend would offer me insights on how to move forward with the group. One thing I did come to realize through this incident was that I did not necessarily have to be the voice that shifted talk or challenged it. I hoped that students would eventually take on that role through the course of the year, but if they did not, I had ways of bringing in challenging voices. In years past when I had students who took what might be seen as a challenging stance, perhaps one that was too narrow or even offensive, I used texts to work through it. Later in the year, I would have such an opportunity.

Unpacking a Second Wobble Moment

When we get into second semester, we typically read the memoir by three lost boys of Sudan titled *They Poured Fire on Us from the Sky* (Deng, Deng, & Ajak, 2005). By the time we reach this text, students are fairly comfortable with various discussion protocols and most have found their voice in the classroom. The text is not easy for them to relate to, considering that they come from mostly secure homes in suburbia, and the three boys in the book face the perils of the bush and genocide.

We work at connecting to the boys through their experiences of coming of age and definitions of courage. This perspective helps students to see themselves in the lives of the Sudanese boys, Alepho, Benson, and Benjamin, but they really have nothing to draw on in regard to surviving impossible odds and being faced with losing all family and home. They read as outsiders, and while they work at sympathizing with the narratives, they cannot truly empathize. At the end of the book, we aim to work through some of the questions it has raised for us as readers who are fairly far removed from the lives of Alepho, Benson, and Benjamin.

Our inquiry usually begins during reading. We raise a number of questions at the end of various sections of the memoir and continue to add to these questions as we finish the book. I have approached the ending in a number of ways each year that I have taught the book. There have been years when students select a question from our list of inquiries and explore it through a research project. I have had students trace motifs and themes we see come up again and again through the book. They then complete a visual representation of the motif or theme and analyze why this particular motif or theme was significant for their reading. During the year of our study, I chose to follow our finishing the book with a whole-class discussion. I thought I might take the class into a similar direction as in the previous years, but the discussion challenged me to rethink our unit of study.

When my 7th period finished reading *They Poured Fire on Us from the Sky*, I asked them to develop discussion questions we would use for our final discussion of the text. I looked across their questions and narrowed them down to the ones I saw come up again and again. Many had asked questions that related to one another and some focused too narrowly on specific parts of the book, so I worked to make them broader.

Prior to our day of discussion, I gave the students the set of questions so they could consider five of them, develop their responses, and support those responses with evidence from the text. The day of the discussion, the desks were in the shape of a large oval around the edges of the trailer walls. I elected to use a protocol that allowed students much say in how long we would pursue one topic and when we would shift to another. We had used this protocol before and students had found it useful. I wanted the students to direct the discussion and have their voices be at the center. I chose a seat outside the oval. As I continued explaining in my narrative . . .

The question that got me wondering what our next step might be in our lesson was: What do you think America's role should be when these terrible things are happening around the world and innocent victims like children are suffering and dying? Students had varying points of view, but many echoed what had been shared before when we'd explored this question while reading the text. Some took an isolationist view, citing issues America had as a defense, others felt it wasn't the U.S. government's job to intervene and that it should focus on domestic issues, and a third cohort felt we needed to help those in need.

What troubled me was one student's response. He went so far as to say that "God helps those who help themselves." I tried desperately not to intervene; this was their discussion and I knew that if I were to step in, I would shut down all dialogue. I waited, hoping that someone would speak against these statements, but few people tried. Once God was brought into the discussion, many sat and nodded. The student next to me gave affirmation to the student's comments by saying, "Yeah, that's true. It's in the Bible." They gave no specific examples for their arguments (except God's will) and that's when I knew I had to take the time to delve into the issues surrounding humanitarian action and foreign policy.

The tension here becomes a question of what really made me uncomfortable about the way this discussion was going and the student's comment. We all enter our classrooms with biases and agendas; sometimes those are very apparent and sometimes they are subtle. The tension developed in this dialogical process of discussion was based in my personal response to the question and the students' responses. My personal stance on the question and then hearing their responses raised a few hairs on the back of my neck. Had I interjected in the discussion, it would have curtailed the conversation and would have established me as the authoritative voice in the discussion, simultaneously squelching what I wanted in my dialogical classroom. I would be no different from the squawking voice demanding they leave the building each afternoon. Although it might have got my agenda across, it would have silenced portions of the room whose agendas did not align with my own.

I do not believe that we can or should disallow biases and agendas in all classrooms, but what the dialogical classroom offers is a way in which to have those agendas and biases voiced, while also listening to and understanding others. Whether a discussion or reading of a text shifts a student's point of view is not really the objective. I did not want to have students "see the light" in regard to their stance around this question. Instead, what made me most uncomfortable was their talking in generalizations and in ways that seemed uninformed or unexamined. I wanted them to have an informed opinion, even if it differed from my own. Knowing that I wanted to continue to work with this group in a dialogical way, I considered my options.

Looking for suggestions on resources, I turned to my media specialists and to the HEN Listserv, which is offered by a professional organization focused on genocide studies. I went to the databases available through our school's media center website and located articles arguing the opposing sides of humanitarian aid and foreign policy. I took this as an opportunity to engage in dialogue and to study persuasive argument.

Armed with all these new resources, we began the conversation on a new day by trying to define *empathy*, *sympathy*, and *apathy*. I did not want them to define the words within the context of a specific text, but just asked what they took the words to mean. They turned to partners and compared their responses. Then we talked as an entire class. I gave three students dictionaries so that we could compare our working definitions with those in the dictionary. Students questioned whether or not one had to have experienced the same sort of thing in order to truly empathize with someone else. Many students felt that you did, but one student was adamant that you didn't. As he challenged other students' ideas, some began to say that perhaps they agreed with him. One student became upset that we weren't arriving at answers but only more questions. I smiled.

I wanted students to arrive at more questions than answers as we made our way through this inquiry. I smiled because I had students truly dialoging with one another over their definitions and their understanding of *empathy*, *apathy*, and *sympathy* instead of just nodding in agreement, as they had in our discussion of foreign policy. I knew the more they shared and questioned, the more they were reflecting on their understanding.

It was also significant to me that they were the ones raising the questions and providing the examples to support their definitions. I could have delivered the definitions and provided the examples for them, but this would have been a passive way to learn. Rather than call on a few students, receive their answers, and then move on to the next activity, I restated what students shared and asked what the whole group thought. As I did so, more hands went up and responses were shared. Students listened to what the people before them said and responded directly. It was not a discussion where everyone just reports out on his or her thoughts and we move on to the next person; we were making meaning together through our dialogue.

Keeping the definitions in mind and our construction of what we felt it meant to be sympathetic, empathetic, and apathetic, we read Virginia Satir's (2003) poem "Making Contact." I asked that they write what they believed Satir's point to be in the poem. We shared these and talked about the idea of being close to someone and what it might mean to be intimate in ways that were not sexual. The word *intimate* was part of one of the definitions we found in the dictionary.

Then we shifted to reading Azad Nafisi's (2005) This I Believe essay, "Mysterious Connections That Link Us Together." As we read, I asked that students make note of where our definitions and understandings of *empathy*, *sympathy*, and *apathy* were explored in her essay. She uses the word *curious* early in the essay and this was also a word that came up in our developing definitions of *empathy*, *sympathy*, and *apathy*. As we read, I completed a read aloud on the overhead, raising questions and making connections to our previous discussion, the reading of the text, and prior readings the students may have done either in our class or during their 9th-grade year. Finally, we ended with a writing assignment that asked students to reflect on the dialogue of the past few class sessions (see Appendix D).

Shifting from a topic that students had little understanding of, or personal connection with, toward an examination of personal response to texts allowed for us to move beyond the generalizations that came up in our discussion around foreign aid and humanitarian action. Rather than forcing them to find the personal in the academic, I attempted to have them clarify their personal understanding and then apply that understanding to academic texts. As we worked our way through our exploration, text complexity increased. As it did so, we moved away from first-person narratives into a silent film, persuasive speeches, and articles from databases arguing both sides of the issues on foreign aid and humanitarian action.

Our next move was to look closely at persuasive argument. We watched the 1989 Oscar-winning short film *Balance* (Lauenstein & Lauenstein, 1989) and discussed it. I brought in copies of Elie Wiesel's speech "The Perils of Indifference" (1999). Again we did a read aloud as a whole group to get started and students finished it for homework. Then we turned to articles. I used the jigsaw protocol to move students through a variety of articles, first on humanitarianism and then on foreign aid. Now, when they discussed the issues they did not make unsubstantiated references or claims but instead used the evidence within the texts for support. I think we continued to raise more questions than we arrived at answers. As a final assignment, they were asked to evaluate where they stood today and how the readings either reaffirmed or challenged their beliefs.

Did the choice of more deeply exploring foreign aid and humanitarian response take additional time that I had not originally factored in when planning our unit? Certainly. In an age when we are heavily influenced by mandates focused around new standards and when we lose more and more of our autonomy in the classroom, this choice may not seem an option at all to many. I could have easily walked away at what I thought would be the end of our unit, the discussion after finishing *They Poured Fire on Us from the Sky,* and been disappointed that students relied on generalizations as a defense against difficult questions. I definitely had the pressure of the end of the semester looming over us and a fear that we were not going to cover all of what I originally intended to do.

If I had chosen just to move on and chalk it up to bad timing or lack of understanding on the part of students, I would have lost an opportunity. We still met the standards, probably more than I had originally planned. We also codeveloped a research project at the end of our exploration. The students felt that others needed to know as much as they did about issues of genocide, humanitarian action, and foreign aid. We planned and organized a project where they would present to peers once their further research was done. Students formed groups based on the topics and issues around what had interested them most from our readings and discussions. We set up a museum-style presentation where their peers moved from exhibit to exhibit while my students shared their findings and answered questions around the artifacts they created.

What had begun as a passive and generalized whole-class discussion turned into a student-centered and student-directed project. They authentically engaged with the material they learned and then shared this knowledge with their peers. The last exhibit was a call to action in which the students provided their audience with ways to act in their communities in regard to refugee families.

Would this have taken place in a top-down, monologic classroom? Would my students have been so engaged with their inquiry and understanding that they would have wanted to share it with as many peers as possible had this not taken place in a dialogical classroom? Would I have been willing to negotiate valuable time so that they could put together a research project like they did in any other setting?

What I believe this wobble moment shows is that a dialogical classroom can achieve things that a monologic classroom cannot and can help students grow in ways no standardized test can. Students can become powerful agents of change by understanding what it means to not only ask questions about their world but also find answers to the questions they collaboratively create within the classroom community.

However, working dialogically takes time, observation, and flexibility. It does not happen easily. When students hear again and again that their voices do not matter or that we just want them to comply with our demands, getting them engaged in a classroom built around dialogical teaching principles can be difficult.

A call for dialogue is also a call for a redistribution of power. Dialogue requires that multiple voices might share in creating meaning, not just one directing students to meaning. It suggests that there might be multiple ways of viewing the world. It does not limit this multiplicity to just one correct answer that can be bubbled in on a Scantron.

Dialogue can also be messy. Opening up a classroom to dialogical teaching practices does not mean that all dialogue will be polite and cooperative; it can also engender frustration for students who become empowered in places that typically view them as powerless. For example, a student in my classroom will be accustomed to having the space to use her voice, to feeling empowered through dialogical processes. Once she leaves my room, the next classroom teacher may not teach from a dialogical stance and should the student insert her voice in this teacher's class, the student runs the risk of being seen as defiant.

A STANDARDS- AND DIALOGUE-DRIVEN CLASSROOM

If we model our classrooms and schools after the loud squawking intercom voice that demands that students follow directions without question or hesitation, we shut down possibilities for open dialogue. Although dialogical classrooms are tension-filled spaces, and not necessarily about everyone seeing eye to eye, they promote growth for both teacher and student. Indeed, the tensions are necessary for that growth to take place. Dialogical classrooms are not passive environments where information is poured into the chute of our students' minds. Dialogical classrooms are not authoritative spaces where all adopt the teacher's agenda and those who do not comply are silenced. Instead, dialogical classrooms are spaces where learners and teacher actively engage in individual and collective meaning making.

I realize the immense amount of pressure teachers face in schools to adapt to the ever-changing landscape of mandates and standards. It would be easier to be the squawking intercom voice and move through the standards without pause. The concern is what it takes away from ourselves as professionals and from our students as learners if we opt for the latter approach. My fear is that growth will not happen and we cannot achieve the interchangeable roles as "teacher-students and students-teacher" as Freire challenges us to live within.

Freire's (1970) observations about the power of dialogue on both the students and the teacher are significant. The reciprocal nature of being in dialogue with students and students being in dialogue with the teacher allows for both parties to become "jointly responsible for a process in which all grow" (p. 80). We see great examples of this dynamic in the work of Jeffrey Duncan-Andrade and Ernest Morrell (2008). In their in-school and out-of-school engagements with students, they illustrate, through example after example, how the roles of student and teacher become interchangeable.

In the current educational climate that we work in, those outside our classrooms—our department chairs, administrators, system superintendents, and policymakers—argue that teachers have a responsibility to ensure growth of our students through the standards. Standardized tests are created to show the growth of our students in relation to their mastery of the standards. In some cases and for many in the not so far off future, our pay will be tied to whether or not our students show growth on standardized testing from one year to the next. The double standard we work within is that we know our students and we will be held to these standards, but we also know that those standards are not enough.

The dialogical classroom, on the surface, may appear as just a place where dialogue occurs between students and teacher. It is a place that is much more than just that. The dialogical classroom may start as just dialogue among people, but to really achieve the true dialogical classroom, it must grow to dialogue with text, with systems, and with the world. In doing this, the student becomes more empowered and more knowledgeable about how she can use her voice. The dialogical classroom is structured around taking critical stances at not only what others say verbally but also what others say in text or in action. In this space, the student becomes more than just a student who has mastered a "standard."

ANGELA'S SUGGESTIONS FOR ACTION

I believe teaching and learning to be vulnerable acts. Like each of the authors of this book, I have to be willing to be vulnerable in the presence of my students. I have to be willing to partake in the exercises and questions with which I am asking them to participate. It is in this tension that I find myself and my students in dialogue. It is uncomfortable for each of us at one point or another, but if I am not willing to enter this vulnerable space with them, our classroom becomes nothing more than the anecdotes about the squawking intercom or (un)inspirational posters plastered on the walls I have described in my chapter. It becomes monologic.

My call to action for other educators is to consider doing the following:

- Find time to be reflective about the tensions in the school and the classroom.
- Be prepared to be challenged in your assumptions about what is actually taking place in the classroom versus what you believe to be happening.
- Connect with a group of colleagues or at least one colleague who will push you in constructive ways as you explore these issues.
- Allow for the voices of differing perspectives to shape the dialogue of your classroom with your students; rely on the texts you bring in to create wobble.

Participating in a group such as ours helped me to look closely at what was and was not taking place, what I assumed and what was actual. For example, I needed my colleagues to push my views in places where I felt finding consensus was necessary in class discussions around particular texts. When I shared the work of my class regarding the excerpt from *A House on Mango Street*, the research team pushed me to question why consensus was what I was after and with whom I wanted the majority to agree. I had to consider carefully the voices of the research team and reflect on my intentions and purposes for developing a dialogic space with my students. Through our dialogue, my purpose for teaching in a dialogic way became more muddled and clear at the same time; it too was a tension-filled space.

As a secondary teacher, I find that it is easy to become isolated. We close our doors and we do our thing. Being in dialogue with students can teach us many things, but unless we bring in the voices of those outside our classroom to really help us examine it, I fear we risk becoming shortsighted and perhaps dogmatic. In conversation with Bob about having students take a critical stance, he challenged me to consider why I might want students to do so. He questioned whether I wanted students to simply adopt my perspective or to be able to better articulate their own after close examination of all the voices presented in our studies. My intentions were with the latter option, but on reflection I wondered if my students felt that were true. It is through dialogue such as this that our practice improves.

Sharing stories from your classroom with colleagues from within and outside your school can bring fuzzy areas of your practice into sharper focus. Asking others to consider those stories in some systematic way will quickly move such storytelling beyond faculty lounge gripe sessions and into richer dialogue about the complexity of teaching.

There is also risk in attempting to ignore the power structures and the voice they attempt to insert. If anything, they must be brought in so that we may question them in critical ways. If we don't raise such questions, who will? How will our students raise such questions if we do not? I cannot take part in a classroom that ignores the structures negatively affecting my students. However, as teachers, we need to rein in our knee-jerk reaction to see as negative and problematic anything that comes from building or district administration. Instead, if we take a dialogical stance on our practices, then we need to pursue all opportunities for such dialogue. Just because the path to dialogue may seem steep or even difficult to perceive at all doesn't mean we shouldn't try. Ultimately, creating better dialogue with those outside our classrooms makes it easier for us to enrich the dialogue within.

CHAPTER 6

Our Future Stories

Bob Fecho and Xiaoli Hong

Recently, Bob interviewed a 1st-year teacher who was applying to the Red Clay Writing Project. Cassie was exuberant about teaching and particularly about engaging with the working-class and working poor African Americans and Latin@s who made up the bulk of the student population of her school. She went on at length about the ways she was using dialogue to help students understand that the rich and vibrant experiences of their lives had merit and worth in the academic world of a high school English classroom. Students were talking to one another, conferencing with her, writing at length, and beginning to see her classroom as a space that welcomed their ideas, critiques, and questions. But when Bob asked Cassie what aspects of her practice she wanted to improve, her face clouded over. She lifted her gaze up to the ceiling and finally she blurted out, "I have 180 students."

Cassie really didn't have to explain anything else. She was teaching in a school where many of the students frequently haven't seen success. She was being held to state and federal standards through a series of exams imposed from those outside her classroom sources. There was, underlying every minute of the school day, an expectation that her students would raise their test scores, and she would be instrumental in and responsible for making those increases happen. And she was to do this with every one of the 180.

You can feel the tug of tensions that Cassie is feeling. She's a new teacher who wants to do well in the eyes of the administration that hired her, so she tries to adhere to the standards and rostering policies of her school. On the other hand, she desires to develop strong teaching and learning relationships with her students. Given the number of students in her teaching load, she feels somewhat compelled to teach in ways that consume less class time and fewer of her own energy resources. However, in her heart she knows that expending time and energy with students results in the acquisition of substantive learning skills and not just superficial gleaning of information. She understands the need for her students to acquire the mainstream codes of academia if they want to realize some future life and career within the economic, scientific, and political communities. Yet she's adamant that such acquisition should not be at the nullification and invalidation of their rich cultural heritages. Perhaps key to all her concerns, Cassie wants to engage in dialogical ways with her students—ways that help them to see learning as a generative act rather than a receptive or even degenerative one—but experiences such pedagogical stances being crowded aside by pressure from outside sources to act in other ways.

We think the vignette about Cassie encapsulates many of the tensions we identified in Chapter 1 and saw evidence of in the wobble moments described by Paige, Lisa, Ian, and Angela. Clearly tensions between policy from more global sources are impinging upon her local decisions as a teacher. The personal experiences, cultures, and desires of Cassie and her students are seeking to find room in the academic expectations that permeate the school. The many stakeholders—administration, students, and Cassie, to name but a few—all want their agendas to be heard and realized. Dominant mainstream middle-class expectations of what counts as learning tug at worldviews of adolescents from worlds figured as more marginalized. With so many students, Cassie vacillates between teaching in expedient ways that do little more than help students pass tests and teaching in ways that enable them to be part of a lifelong process of meaning making. And perhaps not as directly evident, Cassie ponders the question: When policymakers create what can seem like unrelenting standardized testing, is it ethical for her to comply with policy that she considers wrongheaded, perhaps even harmful?

Would that we could wave a wand and get Cassie's class size down to a more manageable number. However, we have no inclination to eliminate the tensions she is feeling. To an extent, those tensions need to be in place. For example, in and of themselves, standards are not inherently evil. Why would we expect to teach without any standards, ones that we as a community have generated and come to accept? Nevertheless, the tensions around standardization have skewed way toward the global side of the spectrum, to the point that, locally, teachers, parents, and students have very little individual input into the content of any set of standards and how that content is best delivered. From our stance, tensions between opposing forces, if both forces can more or less develop a sense of equilibrium, create favorable zones for learning. It's when one of the opposing forces gains too much of an upper hand—when, for instance, policymakers with a more global stance foist national standards and the standardized tests that accompany them on local communities—that tensions go from being generative to becoming degenerative.

Consequently, a subhead for this chapter might be "Dialoguing Within Tensions." Tensions exist in all facets of teaching—in all facets of life—and rather than eliminating tensions, we need to understand what tensions are present and how to maintain some equilibrium between opposing forces that create the tension. How do we best seek some measure of unity in order to embrace some shared ideas and ways of working while valuing and, indeed, fostering individual perspectives and interpretations?

UNPACKING THE TENSIONS ACROSS THE WOBBLE MOMENTS

In Chapter 1, we identified the following six tensions as the most prevalent and insistent within our data:

- globalization and localization
- the personal and the academic
- the conflicting agendas of stakeholders
- the mainstream and the margins
- the ethical and the legal
- the expedient and the desired

Through the remainder of this chapter, we first explore these six tensions in depth by showing how they manifested in the dialogical practices developed by our four teachers. We step back to take this larger view with the intent to explore how tensions help us see the complexities involved in enacting engaged dialogical practice within standards-based educational settings. By unpacking these tensions, we also display how engaged dialogical practice creates a transactional space where different voices, especially the voices of disenfranchised and marginalized students, are heard and collide with one another. Although we mostly focus on the wobble moments contained within the teacher chapters, from time to time we refer to other such moments not shared previously but contained in our data set.

We follow this discussion by planting our discussion firmly in future classrooms. Building from the wobble moments contained within our data, we suggest ways for teachers to (1) position themselves for engaged dialogical practice, (2) develop structures and ways of working that will support such practice, (3) create a practice that can grow within regimes of standardization, and (4) position themselves as agents of change within and beyond the classroom.

Globalization and Localization

Because they teach in standardized schools, all four teachers in our study have had to cope with tensions between global and local influences. More and more—perhaps capping with the Common Core State Standards—the standards by which students, teachers, and schools are judged are imposed at state and national levels. Few if any affordances for local input and flexibility are allowed. The federal government pressures states, whose departments of education pressure district superintendents, who then pass the pressure on to principals, from whom it is dispersed to the faculty. As a result, teachers like Paige, Lisa, Ian, and Angela frequently feel hemmed in and limited by standards that traveled a long time and distance before arriving in their classrooms.

In Lisa's case, this skewing toward conformity was especially acute. Because her school was feeling pressured, the administration elected to place young men whom they labeled "at risk" into situations that could only be labeled humiliating at best. In essence, teachers and students were expected to collude in this process that felt more like denigration than support. Lisa responded by refusing to let herself and Emilio, one of her students, take part in that collusion. However, in doing so, she risked being seen as someone who wasn't a team player, someone who, ironically, put the care of her students over the policies of the school.

We saw in Ian's narrative how his support of undocumented students left him vulnerable to politics beyond his school. For Ian, federal immigration policy has faces and young, creative minds behind those faces. For him, the national debate on immigration comes with names, with families, with stories of struggle, with songs of hope. On a daily basis, Ian is in dialogue with himself and the federal statutes that restrict and even endanger the security of many of the students he teaches. The global border politics of his country are never far out of mind as he greets each student every day.

Moreover, the tension between globalization and localization is apparent when students' limited and largely local experience bumps against social issues and global events. It often happened when the four teachers engaged students in discussions about what it means to be an American or a global citizen or when students introduced topics they learned through various media outside school. Paige described this tension in a wobble moment not discussed in her chapter. She wrote of how three boys in her classroom who "appear to listen to a lot of talk radio and love to engage not so much in dialogue but just debate." They were claiming Barack Obama is not a citizen of United States and the health care bill is going to bankrupt the country. In responding, Paige didn't enter into debate with them. Instead, she suggested other websites and references that these boys might access in order to gain a larger and more informed perspective on these issues.

With the advent of technology that brings the world to us with a mouse click—global access lies literally at our fingertips—discussions that reveal the tension between globalization and localization will become more prevalent in classrooms. Paige, Lisa, Ian, and Angela, when inviting students to the contact zone of different social discourses and cultures from around the world, probably foresee more confusion and uncertainties as possible reactions in the classroom. However, the uncertainties incurred within these tensions also create more opportunities for dialogues with students about how to be a global citizen and how to prepare for instabilities and confusions in an increasingly globalizing world. If the power of the government lies in conformity to policy, the power of individuals in local contexts lies in their stories. We who teach have a far greater ability to get those stories heard than ever before, if only we'll let our fingers do the talking.

The Personal and the Academic

The tension between the personal and the academic is the most frequently seen tension among the narratives in our data set. Teachers experience the tension when their personal values conflict with various requirements in their professional world. For example, in Lisa's narratives, her style of working with students was often described by colleagues as too nurturing and she was questioned by her administrators for not following the standards. She wrote, "To be constantly reminded of the standards and my accountability didn't provide any encouragement to trust my own instincts and push forward." What we see in Lisa's work is a classic conflict between a teacher's wishing to fit into the teaching culture of the school yet wanting to honor her beliefs about instruction. In this case, Lisa's deep-seated belief about building strong relationships with students in order to support their learning placed her in conflict with the cultural ethos of the school, which celebrated rigor above all else.

Another example of the prevailing tensions between the personal and the academic arose when the four teachers intended to connect knowledge learning to students' personal lives. In one of Ian's classes, with the majority of the students being African Americans, he chose to teach many literary works by African American authors because he believed that such texts allowed his African American students to see themselves in and relate to the stories and characters in those books. The intent was to help those students reflect on their lives as part of the course of study. However, some of his students regarded his focus on this literature as a superficial attempt to address issues of race and asked why they needed to read books about Black people.

As Galda and Beach (2001) argued, the classroom itself is a conflicted cultural world. When teachers and students come to school, they all bring their distinct personalities and cultural positions; hence, the tension between the personal and the academic is inherent in classrooms. For both teachers and students, this tension elicits the question, What is the purpose of education/schooling? Although a question like "Which is more valuable in classrooms, the standards or personal learning?" might also be tempting to pose, we wonder if such a question is problematic. Standards—local or national, formal or informal, written or unwritten—will and perhaps always should exist in classrooms. However, so should input from teachers about their experienced-based understandings of what occurs in classrooms and what might be best for students. Entering into dialogue around these tensions is what will allow for an educational context that honors what exists yet positions classrooms in response to current and future needs.

The Conflicting Agendas of Stakeholders

Public and private schools have many interested parties with stakes in the results of education. Businesses want workers with enough education to do the necessary work. Policymakers share some of the goals of business, but are also concerned about developing future leaders. Parents have a wide range of expectations for schools, but frequently connect learning to economic and social ladder climbing. The students themselves bring many differing and often conflicting ideas about why they are in school and what they want from it. All those agendas center themselves in classrooms where teachers try to maintain them within a working equilibrium.

The tension among the conflicting agendas of stakeholders occurs often when a teacher's practice is questioned by parents, administrators, or students. In Paige's case, she was challenged by a parent for talking about NCLB and not covering materials for the next day's test. The parent's email prompted Paige to reflect on her teaching and seriously think about whether her idea of students' learning/engagement applies to all students. In fact, in retrospect, she remembered that "there are students who do not always want to engage in a dialogical classroom and at least claim that they would be better if you just told them what to memorize."

This tension also appeared in Lisa's classroom. As a new high school teacher, she often faced her evaluating administrator's urgings that she "make wise use of time," and her department head frequently reminded her of "the Common Core's emphasis on argumentative and synthesis writing and wasn't interested in hearing how writing a book review might be a way to introduce 10th-graders to that concept." She was torn between her own beliefs about supporting students as they venture into new learning contexts and the administration's expectations of academic rigor above all else.

Perhaps these tensions among stakeholders were most vividly articulated by Angela when she discussed decisions and actions her administration made about managing a large and diverse student population. Through his announcements and in-your-face style, the student resource officer created an authoritarian discourse that may have been effective in keeping the halls clear after school, but also helped to clear any context that might foster dialogue. The cafeteria workers expressed their agenda regarding proper attire that flew in opposition to then current adolescent styles of dress. In her class, sometimes students were open to dialogue on the texts Angela would introduce, and at other times they were more interested in arguing among themselves about slights real and imagined. They also held a diverse range of political and, frequently, unexamined opinions about sociocultural issues. Through it all, Angela continued to construct a dialogical practice that tried to engage all those many stances.

The Common Core State Standards demand much from teachers and hold them accountable, through accompanying standardized tests, for whatever standards students fail. Teachers are supposed to justify their curricula choices and decisions to parents, students, and administrators. Yet it is difficult to satisfy everyone's needs. Hence, the tension between the conflicting agendas of stakeholders encourages all educators to think: Whose voices matter? Why don't we trust teachers to make good decisions as to what counts as quality teaching for the needs of their students? What contexts do more to foster dialogue among these many stakeholders?

The Mainstream and the Margins

Looking across the many wobble moments, the tension between the mainstream and margins was salient when a teacher voice or students' voices were silenced, interrogated, or marginalized. As mentioned above, Lisa's nurturing of her students was seen as outside high school culture by many of her colleagues who deemed such support of students inappropriate and nonrigorous. Perhaps less overtly, but nonetheless evident, Paige felt pressure to cover the standards because she feared she would "get in trouble or be looked down upon by her peers or administrators." In both cases, teachers navigated the need to teach in ways in which they knew their students would thrive and yet also try to assuage concerns raised by administrators and colleagues. That Paige won a Teacher of the Year award at her school and Lisa's talents working with struggling students were digitally recorded for sharing with other teachers somewhat speaks to their success at living within the tensions.

In a wobble moment not discussed in her chapter, Angela, a finalist for Teacher of the Year in her school, was caught off guard when a White student, in discussing a shared text, made his point by imitating what he thought an African American woman sounded like. Worse yet, most of the class responded with laughter rather than admonishment. Angela was particularly concerned that his actions would further silence the few African American students in her class, who already often felt pressed to the edges of many discussions. As a teacher, she sensed a need to do more than shut down this performance, but was less sure about how to go about doing so.

What added to the complexity of the situation was her knowing that earlier in the year the same student had become visibly upset when another student seemed to brand all Muslims as terrorists. She wondered how he could be sensitive to the representation of one group but not to that of another. And she wondered how best to address the issues as a class.

Bakhtin's concepts of centripetal and centrifugal forces render the tension between the mainstream and the margins quite natural and common. Humans are always tugged simultaneously by centralizing forces like mainstream social discourses and individualizing forces like our own personal values. Whereas teachers and students grapple with the two forces through thinking about whether and how to fit in or retain personal uniqueness, the struggle between the mainstream and the margin also invites thoughts about how teachers and educators can promote multiple perspectives and respect for others in schools.

The Ethical and the Legal

In Dr. Martin Luther King Jr.'s famous essay "Letter from a Birmingham Jail," King (1963b) argued the difference between what is legal and what is moral in his discussion of just and unjust laws. According to King, citizens have a legal and moral responsibility to obey a law that is just—one that treats all fairly and uplifts humanity. Flipping the coin, King argued that citizens have an equally moral responsibility to *disobey* an unjust law—one that is out of harmony with moral thought and seeks to degrade rather than uplift. Apartheid in South Africa, Jim Crow laws in the segregated South, the horrors of the Holocaust, and the interment of Japanese Americans during World War II were all acts committed within the boundaries of the law. Few of us today would see those laws as just, and we honor as heroes those who fought against those legal abominations.

Many in teaching consider the No Child Left Behind Act to be an unjust law. Those who oppose it argue that its mandate of what appears to be unrelenting testing, its narrow view of what counts as necessary literacy instruction, its measures of accountability without much regard for local voice and interpretation, and its lack of adequate financial support for ending funding inequities creates a learning context that diminishes rather than enlivens classroom learning. As such, Paige, Lisa, Ian, and Angela struggle daily within institutions that support the injustices of this law. In some ways, all their wobble moments—if not through blunt appraisal then through multiple allusions—address this daily struggle to be more just within an unjust system.

Ian's narratives, perhaps, speak most directly to the presence of tension between that which is legal and that which is ethical. His involvement with undocumented students makes him seemingly a person who disregards law and plays a partisan political role in schools; however, his support of those students is based on what he believes is ethically right and is what a good citizen of the United States should do. Despite being criticized by some observers as being ethically or legally suspect, Ian has continued to rigorously educate all the students who enter his classroom, regardless of how the law chooses to regard their citizenship status.

Although such efforts on his part have resulted in honors from the University of Georgia and the University of Arizona, it is his dialogical relationship with his students that sustains his willingness to work within these tensions. The tension between the ethical and the legal in Ian's case calls forth such questions of practice as *What is the role of a teacher?* and *Can teachers be political advocates in classrooms?* However, most important, Ian's narratives cause us to examine the importance and significance of dialogue in the presence of inequity and injustice.

The Expedient and the Desired

Throughout our discussions of the narratives, time and again, the teachers on the research team indicated decision moments when the pressure to make sure the content deemed necessary to meet the standards was being covered bumped against their desire and that of the students to probe more deeply into subject matter. We were particular in our choice of words in that last sentence: We believe too often course content, as Paige asserted, is merely *covered* rather than learned and taught with depth and complexity. Memorizing the concept of *irony* off a list of literary terms and assessing understanding by a multiple choice quiz is no substitute for reading, discussing, and writing about multiple literary texts in which irony plays a large role. Yet, on a day-to-day basis, all teachers are faced with whether to opt for the expedient former or desired latter.

The tension between the expedient and the desired stands out when teachers' beliefs of what counts as good learning for students have to be put aside for attending to the requirements of standardized testing. In Ian's chapter, the way he prepared his students for the state writing test is a good example with which to illustrate the tension. During the short writing workshop, he had to bludgeon his students with standard writing practice that emphasized form, structure, and syntax. Although he knew that such an approach would most likely enable more students to pass the state writing test, he also knew it would do little to help students to view writing as a worthwhile skill and joyful tool for their lives.

Another example can be seen in one of Angela's narratives. When she involved her students in discussing several questions about how one can truly empathize with someone else, one student became upset that they weren't arriving at answers but were producing more questions. The student probably saw answers as an expedient way of finishing Angela's require- ment, while her desired goal was to open up students' critical thinking skills. Angela's experience relates to Paige's experience in which both a student and a parent raised questions about a discussion on NCLB that they thought was less necessary than using the time to complete a graphic organizer.

As in all the tensions discussed in this chapter, we aren't arguing that one or the other of the opposing forces is the better one. Time is the enemy in classrooms, and teachers need to be aware of how they use time and mindful of using it well. Going into too much depth on a teaching unit can leave other substantive subject matter severely wanting for time, just as metaphorically walking students by essential ideas can stunt students' progress as learners. Our concern remains focused on the need to avoid the skewing of these tensions too far to either side of the continuum, which currently worries us when it comes to classrooms in standardized schools being too dominated by the expedient. Ultimately we ask whether teachers can achieve their desired goal of a more engaged dialogical practice while also fulfilling the requirements in Common Core State Standards.

WHAT CAN WE LEARN FROM THESE TENSIONS?

It seems helpful at this point to remind ourselves that the tensions we've identified can be found in all classrooms, not just those exploring dialogical practice. By forgetting this point, it might appear to some that dialogical teaching practice is daunting and packed with difficulties. To complicate the matter more, in many of the cases discussed herein, several tensions are tan- gled into one moment, making the situation much more complicated. For example, in Ian's case with the Jewish caricature, there were the tensions be- tween the personal and the academic, globalization and localization, and the mainstream and the margins. Likewise, when Lisa was constantly questioned by her evaluating administrators, she also experienced several tensions—the personal and the academic, the mainstream and the margins, the conflicting agendas of stakeholders, and the expedient and the desired.

So we reiterate: These tensions are not created by dialogical teaching practices. Instead, they inherently exist in all classrooms. The tension be- tween globalization and localization is always present in a world heading toward globalization. The tension between the personal and academic is there because we are all raised in different cultural contexts that prompt us to act in certain ways, and the same applies to the tensions between the different agendas of stakeholders. The Common Core State Standards build a situation in which teachers constantly need to consider what they need to cover before they engage students in other curricular contents.

What engaged dialogical practice does do is bring these tensions to the surface by enabling people to feel them and think about how to deal with them. If we look back carefully at the wobble moments, these tensions, while causing teachers, students, and other participants discomfort, also generate opportunities for deepening dialogue, either between teachers and students or self-dialogues within teachers' and students' minds. It is within tensions that we seek to construct new understanding about our students, schools, and the entire educational system.

For instance, in Paige's case with the parent's email, while she felt emotionally hurt and threatened, the email also compelled her to reflect on many questions: How do we meet the needs of different stakeholders? What counts as useful learning? How do we define engagement in classrooms? Also, when we, as a research team, read and relived her wobble moment, we were galvanized by her piece and proposed issues related to dialogical teaching practice: Is dialogical teaching practice good for every student? How do we teach what we are supposed to teach but account for what our interests are? All these questions and ideas will continue to propel Paige, as she performs dialogical teaching practices, and us, the research team, even after the whole project is finished. As Bakhtin (1981) argued, understanding and responses are "dialectically merged and mutually condition each other" (p. 282). It is through understanding and responding to these tensions that we go on an eternal process of regeneration.

It is also within these tensions that we begin to hear those voices that oftentimes are marginalized and disenfranchised. For example, when the Latino and African American students in Ian's class were engaged in a discussion of power and violence related to their daily lives, the district administrator walked in to check the Common Core State Standards covered that day. Despite the tensions of being called into account looming over them, it was within this moment that these students were able to make their voices heard by asking, "Mr. Altman, why the fuck they do that?" We saw in parallel how Ian and his students were engaged with their classroom dialogue and simultaneously annoyed by the administrator's interruption.

Maxine Greene stated, "We have reached a moment in history when teaching and learning, if they are to happen meaningfully, must happen on the verge" (as cited in Enciso, 1994, p. 532). The wobble moment is like a verge in which students can construct meaning when their own daily lives, often dismissed in school, collide with the giant ship of Common Core State Standards. Therefore, tensions create a transactional space where marginalized voices from students and teachers are able to dialogue with administrators, policymakers, and other stakeholders in the educational systems.

The tensions, brought to our attention in the chapters written by Angela, Ian, Lisa, and Paige, showed us the complexities when teachers enact dialogical teaching practice within standards-based settings through dialogical teaching practices, and the way the educational structure sometimes deters or inhibits dialogue with students and teachers. Moreover, these tensions are generative and indicate pathways for growing our understandings about schools, education, and the entire society. They open us to more possibilities while encouraging people to travel into and dialogue through contradictions, confusions, and uncertainties.

Creating a Framework for Engaged Dialogical Practice

The way to a dialogical classroom is not made through clever mnemonics, easy-to-remember acronyms, or step-by-step activities. We don't even wish that it were. Teaching is a complex activity. As David Snowden and Mary Boone (2007) argued, complexity doesn't lend itself to solutions, let alone easy solutions. Which is not to say that dialogical teaching—or any teaching, for that matter—is a useless and aimless activity. Instead, we believe that the work done in classrooms is an ongoing and reflective process that remains in a perpetual state of flux, refinement, and challenge. As such, classrooms remain sites of unpredictability and uncertainty, which also makes them sites of great possibility for substantive and relevant learning.

So what we offer in lieu of those mnemonics, acronyms, and activities is a framework from which you can build your engaged dialogical practice, one that reflects your contexts, your students, your experiences, and your personality. What follows is a discussion of how to position yourself for dialogical practice, what structures and ways of working are often conducive to such practice, how to approach the standardization particulars of your school, and what it means to position yourself as an agent of change.

Don't think of these discussions as a recipe for a dialogical practice. Instead, see them as a menu in process. As with any menu, there will be many ideas discussed that may catch your eye, but only some that you'll actually sample. Of course, there'll be some that won't appeal to you at all. And, as in any menu, there might be items that you wish were there but aren't, or for which you want to substitute one thing for another. We hope that's the case, for then the dialogue has already begun.

Positioning Yourself for Engaged Dialogical Practice

If you think about how Paige, Lisa, Ian, and Angela have positioned themselves to work in dialogical ways, a few stances stand out across the group. To start, they all grasp that wobble is a state of grace (Fecho, 2011a). Not only do they expect the belief systems of their students to wobble; they expect theirs to wobble as well. They also fervently wish that other educational stakeholders—administration, parents, business leaders, and policymakers, to name but a few—would open themselves to wobble. Again, wobble is not change but an indication that change is in the offing, attention must be paid, heed given. Wobble creates a sense of uncertainty; the ground beneath your feet is more unsteady than it has been.

By acknowledging wobble, we as learners, as teachers, as inquirers, as questioners, as humans in search of meaning open ourselves to dialogue. Such acknowledgment of wobble in your belief system does not necessarily mean that you're abandoning those beliefs for another set of beliefs, although that could happen. What it does mean is that you've opened yourself to looking more closely at what's occurring there, to take in other perspectives on possible responses, and to try to better understand the implications of your responses. The upshot might just be generating more thoughtful reasons for believing what you already believe. But even that state of affairs is a significant change from your stance prior to acknowledging wobble.

When Angela wonders if she inserts too much of her leftist agenda into class discussion, when Ian questions whether he wants to always teach in dialogical ways, when Lisa worries that at times she confuses her mothering and teaching life roles, and when Paige thoughtfully considers what students she may not be reaching with her instruction, each is acknowledging wobble and setting themselves up to dialogue through the uncertainty. When some event in their classroom caught their attention, some new school policy made them gasp, or the actions of some student left them confused, they naturally resorted to story and questions to unpack the nuances of their practices. The oral inquiry process (OIP) we used (see Appendix B) only formalized processes that these four teachers already had in place.

Practice for Paige, Lisa, Ian, and Angela is an ongoing exploration of the context in which they teach, not just the space within their classroom walls. In keeping with this idea, we've tried throughout the book to use some variation of *engaged dialogical practice* rather than using *dialogical pedagogy* or *dialogical teaching*. The latter two terms tend to imply only what occurs within classrooms and even then only what directly influences instruction. However, it's our stance that if teachers embrace dialogical practice, they need to embrace dialogue writ large. Just as Ian positioned himself to dialogue with legislators, despite their unwillingness to dialogue meaningfully with him, and Paige considered the importance of dialoguing with parents, we argue that enacting dialogical practice requires positioning oneself to be open to dialogue, wherever one may find it.

Developing Structures and Ways of Working

Flat out, we believe that all teachers can work in dialogical ways no matter what structures surround them. That noted, we also firmly believe that some structures—class size, room size and arrangement, length of class periods, degrees of curricular and instructional autonomy, and tech support, for example—when taken into account can markedly enhance any teacher's ability to engage in dialogical practice. If teachers are in a classroom in which 32 students and the furniture needed to accommodate those students are compressed into a tiny room, small-group and even large-group discussions become more difficult because the structures prevent easy reconfigurations of the room to support dialogue.

Yet it can be done. We won't sell you a bill of goods and say such a setup makes it easy to teach in dialogical ways, but if the belief in the stance is strong, there are ways to make it work. Similarly, engaged dialogical practice is not just for the "advanced" classes. In fact, it generally saddens us when otherwise smart and caring teachers, upon getting excited about dialogical practice, announce they can't wait to try it with their advanced sections. By all means do that, but also by all means enact dialogical practice with all your students, no matter what their supposed "ability." One defining characteristic of the work done by the four teachers in the study is that students who have been less successful and thus marginalized by schooling tend to blossom academically through dialogical engagement.

During this study, Angela was teaching in a windowless, double-wide trailer, the long and narrow construction of which forced her to place desks in an eight-across, four-deep matrix, the desk behind bumping the desk before it. Although she taught a range of classes, Angela chose to write about a 10th-grade class that was considered part of the college preparatory track at her school. In the hierarchy of the school's tracking system, despite the glorified name, the college prep track was considered to be the bottom track, and too many teachers brought similar lowered expectations to those classes. In addition, the school ran class periods that were 50 minutes in length, and being in a trailer parked behind the school, students had to literally exit the main building to get to Angela's classroom.

It would be hard to think of a more daunting set of structures in which to attempt engaged dialogical practice. Yet Angela did more than attempt such work; she found ways to often make it thrive. Despite the cramped conditions, Angela routinely and effectively organized small-group discussions. In spite of the length of the trailer, which placed students in row 1 quite distant from students in row 8, she orchestrated lively whole-group discussions that built out of the small-group work. If at times the short class periods killed momentum on a project from one day to the next, through persistent reconnecting to the dialogical center of the work, she helped students bridge the work day to day, week to week, and month to month.

Part of this persistent reconnecting was Angela's varied use of teaching protocols, which are really just thoughtful frameworks for engaging learners, and which can be adapted in many ways to fit classroom needs. In Angela's chapter she alluded to one such protocol that created opportunities for students to maintain and then eventually change the topic of discussion. As she reported:

> For the discussion, the classroom was set up in one large oval (can't get a circle in the trailer). Students led the discussion and showed their interest in carrying on with a topic by holding up one finger. If they wanted to be called on to change the topic, they held up two fingers. After each student shared and built upon what someone else had said, they would look around the room and call on someone based on the number. If ones still were raised, they had to call on the ones. They could only call on a two if no ones existed. We have used this discussion protocol before and students were familiar with how to engage in the discussion. They have expressed that they like this form of discussion.

Protocols like this one support dialogical practice. Rather than creating a restrictive structure that minimizes engagement, they generate a structure from which dialogue and learning can build. The good news is that many excellent protocols can be found online (for example, see the National School Reform Faculty [2014] site). In general, when shopping for a protocol, look for ones that create opportunities for wide engagement and that encourage higher-order thinking skills. Shop smart—all protocols aren't created equal in terms of their dialogical support—and freely adapt to your context.

In many ways, structures that enable dialogical practice flow from common sense. Engaging 20 students is generally easier than engaging 30 students. Working with 90 minutes of time, to allow a few connected activities to weave together, is preferable to 50 minutes and having to pick up a thread the next day. Rooms large enough to allow for a number of furniture layouts (circles, small groups, work stations, horseshoes, amphitheaters, and the like) do much more to enhance dialogical practice than do crowded, small rooms. Having school and central administration willing to create and sustain such structures is almost too invaluable for words.

Although all these structures are conducive to dialogical practice, perhaps the most critical structure resides in the minds of teachers. As we illustrated above, Angela had many structures working against her; still she managed to continually find ways to engage her students dialogically. She is perhaps the most extreme example, but Ian, Lisa, and Paige navigated any number of structural challenges themselves. However, in the end, the structure that mattered most was that of their belief systems. To a person, all four of them held to the belief that students need to deeply engage ideas from a range of perspectives and toward nuanced and critical reasoning. Beginning with that structural understanding, it just remained for each of them to find the best way to work dialogically within her or his context.

Working Within Standardized Schools

Who doesn't, in some way to some degree, work within a standardized school? Blessings upon those where such standardization lives a more dialogical existence with individual innovation and initiative. Hopefully, more teachers enjoy such circumstances than don't, but our informal survey of news reports, the education literature, and teacher anecdotes tell us a different tale. It seems to us that too many teachers feel hemmed in and constrained by the forces of standardization. They chafe at how instruction around standards is too often mandated in narrow and restrictive ways. We hope our assessment is off the mark, but we doubt that it is.

There is nothing antithetical regarding standards and dialogical practice. One does not preclude the other. Rich and carefully considered performance standards and rich and carefully considered dialogical practice, in many ways, are mutually enhancing. One of the many goals of dialogical practice is to provide learners multiple opportunities to analyze, classify, critique, research, prioritize, argue, defend, reflect, and enact; in other words, a dialogical practice is well positioned to engage students and teachers in a full range of higher-order performance skills that any strong set of standards offers.

What must be interrupted, however, is the tendency for schools to restrict teachers to a one-standard-a-day mentality. Doing so leads to a direct teaching of the standards that is too often decontextualized and superficial. Such atomization of the standards tends, from our stance, to minimize rather than substantiate them. They get lost in a parade of incoherence. Instead, schools should provide ample time before the start of and during the school year for grade groups or departments to sit down with the standards and to consider how they can be clustered within ongoing dialogical projects.

To do this clustering requires somewhat of a wobble in mindset. Rather than thinking about how to teach a certain standard, teachers should develop substantive inquiries based on essential questions (Coalition of Essential Schools, 2015). Such projects should unite personal experience with academic craft, encourage access to multiple perspectives, involve thoughtful engagement across time and space, and create opportunities for substantive meaning making (Fecho, 2011b).

Once a dialogical project is outlined, teachers can than look at the standards and consider which ones can be effectively taught and reinforced through use within the work of the project. Working this way encourages teachers to dialogue with one another about what certain standards are trying to achieve, how standards connect to one another, and what standards might need more support in order to help students gain competency. Perhaps most critical, such an approach honors the importance of standards, but not at the expense of coordinated and cohesive instruction.

Angela's use of an essential question—what does it mean to be a citizen of the world—sets both her and her students up for working dialogically to meet several standards across time. Using the question as a focus, she engages her students with texts that provoke questions and dialogue. To help connect their responses, Angela involves her students with several small-stakes activities—mostly done in school over a class period or two—that lead to higher-stakes projects, tasks that take several days or even weeks to complete. Across that time, students are reading in thoughtful and critical ways, making meaning through writing and discussion, gaining deeper understandings of genre, learning how to listen to one another with intention, and generally getting experience that helps them to meet standards.

In approaching the meeting of standards through dialogical projects, it's important for teachers to have metadiscussions in their classrooms. As Bob pointed out in a book based on his high school teaching experience, students were very engaged in the work and learning of his inquiry-based classroom; however, some students wondered, given the lack of worksheets and grammar drills, when they were going to start doing English. Bob, at this point, would get a dialogue moving by asking the class, "Well, is this English?" As various voices chimed in with the range of activities engaged and skills being taught, students and Bob became more aware of how comprehensive the learning had been and, with its being embedded in substantive work, how much more meaningful it was. But those positives wouldn't have been noted if the metadialogue—the thinking about the thinking—hadn't occurred (Fecho, 2004).

Positioning Yourself as an Agent of Change

At some instance, maybe consciously or maybe not, Paige, Lisa, Ian, and Angela positioned themselves as agents of change within their schools and within their communities. There are numerous examples in their chapters of their having done so. Angela strolled her school and questioned messages being sent to students; Ian interceded when a state legislator confronted an undocumented student; Lisa, despite doubts, continued to teach in dialogical ways that went counter to the culture of the school; and Paige inserted graphica, primary texts, and modern essays into her social studies curriculum, which got students beyond the traditional history textbook.

We don't see these examples as acts of defiance; we see them as acts of dialogue. In teaching as they do, these teachers are offering their practices as spaces in which a larger dialogue about teaching and learning can take place. None of them are starting revolutions, but all are starting ongoing engagement with ideas worth unpacking, considering, reflecting upon, and talking about. Each of them understands that their greatest locus of control resides within themselves and in the classrooms where they daily transact with students. Although they might get involved in movements that champion larger change efforts, they recognize that they can't always wait for such change to manifest. Instead, they author change in their own practices and invite others to share in their dialogues with those practices.

We hope that teachers will see themselves as agents of change and their classrooms as sites of change. As evidenced by our four teachers, being a change agent does not necessarily mean that you are putting your career and livelihood at risk. Instead, it means caring enough about what happens in your school to teach in ways that interrupt unthinking compliance. It means exploring what you are doing in your teaching and calling it into question, if only to better understand why you do what you do. It means inviting other teachers into your classroom to get their perspective and then opening a dialogue about the many complexities of instruction. It means being in the moment, mindful, heedful, having your head in the game and your heart in the outcome. Being an agent of change doesn't mean that you have the answers; it means that you have the questions. And it means that you're willing to dialogue with others in pursuit of positive responses to those questions.

LAST STORIES

On the one hand, this section is the end of our collection of stories. On the other hand, it's really the start of our next dialogical response. Toward that effort, we need to address a tone that crept into all the chapters written by the four teachers. At some point, in each of those chapters, anger is evident. While being walked around her school, we noted the anger in Angela's words as she related the way too many students were brought under suspicion by messages the school authorities sent. Ian somehow found a way to control himself as the state legislator bullied his student, but his anger was palpable. A similar anger bubbled just below the surface of Lisa's words as she told of needing to step in before seeing her student Emilio humiliated. For her part, Paige expressed frustration as her efforts to engage her students in rich dialogue seemed to be misunderstood and certainly unappreciated by a parent.

None of these teachers are arrogant rabble-rousers. However, they all care deeply about the work they do and the students they teach. They believe enough in dialogue to know that they don't have all the answers, but they equally believe that administrators and policymakers don't have all the answers either. Instead, if all education stakeholders were to enter into an ongoing dialogue around teaching and learning—one that recognized and valued all voices at the table—more of the inequities that drag so many marginalized students down would become less of a factor in their lives.

Paige, Lisa, Ian, and Angela have earned their anger. They have seen the voices of teachers eroded over the first 15 years of this century as rigid standardization has taken hold. They have experienced the professionalism of teachers being shunted to the margins of education by paced curricula and too many standardized tests. They know what narrow visions of literacy and overzealous control of what is taught and how it is taught have meant for all students in their classrooms, but particularly those students whose status as a minority casts them under an educational shadow. Their anger is real; their anger is justified.

If the education community is smart, they'll acknowledge that anger and try to understand where it comes from and why it has manifested. Departments of education should ask, "Why are teachers who are doing such great work in classrooms so angry?" State legislators should wonder about the top-down structures that dominate too many schools and worry how that domination silences those who are closest to students and know firsthand what is happening in classrooms. Parents should sense the anger and ask what they can do to advocate for dialogue in the name of creating better education for their children.

What we've outlined isn't just a case of four angry teachers. We on the team that completed this study and wrote this book can't believe that these four thoughtful and accomplished teachers we've profiled are the only ones who are angry about the lack of substantive dialogue within schools. Surely such anger has already motivated many creative and innovative teachers to leave the classroom. Just as surely such anger will continue to motivate more to leave. If the aim of current policy is to rid schools of teachers who bring insight and care with them on a daily basis, we suspect that policy is far too effective.

Which brings us back to Cassie, the relatively new teacher we profiled at the start of this chapter. We wrote this book for her and others like her. Cassie wants to believe she can teach in dialogical ways that provide opportunities for her and her students to make meaning of the texts of their lives. But, after only 1 year, she's already sensing that structures in her school collude against her doing so. Much too quickly, Cassie is being grabbed by creeping weeds of doubt that want to choke off her budding dialogical practice.

But Cassie already possesses the key structure for moving forward: She believes that teaching in dialogical ways in a standardized school is possible. She intuits that the standards imposed from outside her classroom can be augmented and enhanced by the higher teaching standards to which she holds herself. She is self-aware of her capacities to create dialogical opportunities and is just looking for some dialogical support to get her through the uncertainties.

In response, we offer the experiences of Paige, Lisa, Ian, and Angela. These veteran teachers have found ways to straddle the gap between the state and national standards for which they are held accountable and the higher-level, personal standards to which they hold themselves accountable. Paige still manages to teach in dialogical ways despite doublethink messages sent by school and district administration. Ian positions himself in the political center between questionable state immigration policy and the needs of undocumented students. Lisa holds a mirror up to her school and her practice as she champions the importance of strong educational relationships. Angela contends with the antidialogical messages sent by school authorities while simultaneously finding ways to run a very pro-dialogical classroom.

Certainly, the main reason these teachers we've profiled are willing to work within these tensions is because they believe it's best for the students they teach. They expect from their students what national standards only hint at. And more often than not, their students rise to those elevated expectations. However, Paige, Lisa, Ian, and Angela also know that by implementing and sharing their dialogical practices, they'll provide for Cassie and others like her a dialogical path down which these less experienced teachers will find the timber for the framework on which to build their own dialogical classrooms. To these teachers we say, borrowing the words and sentiment from *Star Trek*'s Jean-Luc Picard, "Make it so."

Research Design

The research study was designed and implemented collaboratively by a university researcher and teacher educator (Bob), two university doctoral students (Michelle and Xiaoli), and four secondary teachers (Paige, Lisa, Ian, and Angela). It was a qualitative study designed to be as dialogical as we could make it.

Data Collection

Paige, Lisa, Ian, and Angela spent the better part of a school year writing about key events in their attempts at dialogical practice within the policy frameworks of their respective schools. At a pace of two to three entries a month, they reflected on how they decided what to teach, how to approach the chosen subject matter, and how they negotiated those decisions with educational stakeholders. The team agreed that the focus of the writing should be wobble moments that the teachers felt reflected the dialogical issues we were pursuing. All entries were placed on a common wiki that was created specifically for the study.

Bob, Michelle, and Xiaoli augmented the descriptions of wobble moments with classroom observations that occurred on a similar two-to-three-per-month pace. These observations were designed with the intent of bringing another perspective to the classroom—a second story, if you will. Again, we didn't deem it necessary for the participants to coordinate their writing choices with our observations, leaving the teachers free to write about events of significance to them. As we moved into spring, Lisa also added narratives from her middle school classroom to our research wiki but, largely due to crowded schedules, was not observed.

Data Analysis

For analysis of the wobble moment descriptions, the seven of us met monthly beginning in October 2011 and extending through May 2012. We decided to use oral inquiry processes, particularly the descriptive review, as inspirations for our collaboration (Himley with Carini, 2000).

Although our work wasn't focused on one child, as in a descriptive review, we wanted to honor that process's emphasis on (1) description before evaluation, (2) encouragement of multiple perspectives, (3) inclusion of all participants, and (4) dialogue over debate. We thus evolved a process whereby each teacher researcher presented a wobble moment description by reading it aloud to the group, and the remaining members of the research team responded to that description using three questions as guides: (1) What stood out for you in this narrative? (2) What connections did you make to the narrative? and (3) What issues did it raise for you about dialogical pedagogy? (see Appendix B for a step-by-step explanation of the oral inquiry process).

Our responses were conducted similar to that of a whip-around classroom activity in that we would circle the table with each of us giving one response for a particular question until all responses were exhausted. The presenter would then summarize our responses and we'd move to the next set. This process of oral inquiry was followed by a general discussion of the issues and ideas raised by the protocol. Over the course of the academic year, we made one exception to that process: Our monthly meeting in February 2012 was devoted to a more open dialogue about our experiences to date.

In the year that followed, the team looked for similar and discrepant cases across the data with the intent of identifying tensions that were transacting in these classrooms. As noted throughout the book, those tensions—globalization and localization, the personal and the academic, the conflicting agendas of stakeholders, the mainstream and the margins, the ethical and the legal, the expedient and the desired—although not the only tensions that exist in any classroom, were the ones that were most prevalent and insistent in the classrooms of our four teachers.

Oral Inquiry Process

1. One teacher shares a wobble moment description with the team.
2. Team asks clarifying questions (e.g., "What were the racial demographics of the classroom?").
3. Team writes in response to three Qs:
   a. What stood out in this narrative?
   b. What connections did you make to this narrative?
   c. What issues did you identify in this narrative?
4. Team responds to first question in whip-around fashion (one response per participant per turn) with teacher who presented the description taking notes, but not talking.
5. Team continues responding in turn to first question until all responses are exhausted.
6. Teacher who presented the description organizes the responses on the fly and shares (e.g., "A number of responders mentioned how similar situations in their classrooms caused some students to feel silenced").
7. Steps 4–6 are repeated for questions b and c.
8. Team finishes with open discussion.
9. Cautions and notes:
   a. Newcomers to this protocol may find the controlled response artificial at first because they are used to jumping in when they want to talk. However, following the protocol ensures that all voices have the opportunity to contribute and that multiple perspectives get placed on the table.
   b. It's important that the teacher who is sharing the wobble moment remains silent during the response portion of the protocol. Doing so creates a situation where the teacher can completely focus on the range of response and not feel a need to clarify or defend his or her actions.
   c. Responses should be shared in a positive and supportive manner.
   d. Clarifying questions should be just that (see example above) and not a veiled attempt to suggest some form of action (e.g., "Have you thought about calling the parent?")

Questions from the Readings in Angela Dean's Class

This first set of questions was developed by Angela's students:

- How would you feel if there was "nowhere" in the world for you? Have you ever felt that way?
- How do you think you might react to life in Kakuma? Could you survive in an environment as harsh as this? What do you think you could put up with? What would be your breaking point?
- If put in Benjamin's shoes, what would you do to try and get to Kakuma?
- How different might your relationships in your family be if you experienced what they have?
- Can determination save you from death?
- The boys have traveled thousands of miles. How far have they traveled in maturity? Who do you believe has come the furthest and why?
- How have the boys changed since the beginning of the book? For the good and the bad?
- Do the actions of the soldiers surprise you? What reasons might they have for the way they treat the boys?
- Why do the host countries seem to resent the refugees' presence?
- Would you be able to leave companions/family behind for a new start?
- Why were the police so cruel and violent?
- The fact that Alepho has the chance to go to America forces him to study harder. What has motivated you to do something more or work harder? How did that turn out?
- Does hearing about America from their points of view change the way you look at our country?

Angela gave her students this second set of questions to help them to consider broader ideas that the text challenged all of them to consider:

- What does the African proverb at the beginning of the book, "When two elephants fight, it is the grass that gets trampled," mean to you?

- This book was dedicated to Monyde. What does he symbolize?

- These boys lost their homes and their families, were thrust into terrible suffering, and saw things we as adults never experience. What do you think made them want to keep going at times when it would have been so easy to just sit under a tree and leave all that pain?

- Education seemed to be very important to the lost boys. What do you think sparked that desire?

- Why do you think the editor, Judy A. Bernstein, opens the memoir with an introduction and ends it with an epilogue?

- What did you find surprising about the information introduced in this book?

- How has reading *They Poured Fire* changed your ideas about the people and country of Sudan?

- Is the situation in Sudan a war or genocide? When should a conflict be considered just a war and when does it become a genocide? Why?

- What do you think America's role should be when these terrible things are happening around the world and innocent victims like children are suffering and dying?

- Is your lasting impression of *They Poured Fire* one of hope or of despair?

Writing Assignment from Angela Dean's Class

Response:

- What do you interpret the last two paragraphs of this essay to mean? How does it connect to the poem "Making Contact" by Virginia Satir?

- What has been your experience reading *They Poured Fire on Us from the Sky* and watching "Lost Boys from Sudan" (2004)? In what ways do you feel you've connected with the boys and their lives? Have you found yourself being empathetic or sympathetic? What is the difference and why do think you feel the way you do?

- You've read about and studied genocide before and you'll read about and study it again. What does each experience mean to you? Does it bring you closer to understanding? Does it carry you farther away? Does it reaffirm your beliefs in humanity? Does it challenge them? Does it give you hope or does it destroy hope? Does it make you wonder what responsibilities we have for one another? Does it make you want to bury your head in sand?

References

Adichie, C. N. (2009). The danger of a single story. *Technology, Entertainment, Design*. Retrieved from www.ted.com/talks/chimamanda_adichie_the_danger_of_a_single_story

Altman, I. (2011, November 9). Let my people go. *The Flagpole*. Retrieved from issuu.com/flagpolemagazine/docs/ fp111109

Anonymous, & Smith, J. D. (2009). *The Mahabharata*. London, UK: Penguin Books.

Apple, M. W. (2001). *Educating the "right" way: Markets, standards, God, and inequality*. New York, NY: Routledge Falmer.

Bakhtin, M. (1981). Discourse in the novel. In M. Holquist (Ed.), *The dialogic imagination: Four essays* (C. Emerson & M. Holquist, Trans.) (pp. 259–422). Austin, TX: University of Texas Press.

Bakhtin, M. (1984). *Problems of Dostoevsky's poetics* (C. Emerson, Ed. & Trans.). Minneapolis, MN: University of Minnesota Press.

Bakhtin, M. (1986). *Speech genres and other late essays* (C. Emerson & M. Holquist, Eds., V. McGee, Trans.). Austin, TX: University of Texas Press.

Bidwell, A. (2014, August 20). Common Core support in free fall. *U.S. News and World Report*. Retrieved from www.usnews.com/news/articles/2014/08/20/common-core-support-waning-most-now-oppose-standards-national-surveys-show

Bruner, J. (2004). Life as narrative. *Social Research*, 71(3), 691–710.

Coalition of Essential Schools. (2015). Essential questions. Retrieved from essential-schools.org/benchmarks/ essential-questions

Chilcott, L. (Producer) & Guggenheim, D. (Director). (2010). *Waiting for Superman*. United States: Paramount Vantage.

Cisneros, S. (1991). *The house on Mango Street*. New York, NY: Vintage Books.

Clandinin, D. J., & Connelly, F. M. (2000). *Narrative inquiry: Experience and story in qualitative research*. San Francisco, CA: Jossey-Bass.

Clifton, L. (1987). Homage to my hips. *Good woman: Poems and a memoir 1969–1980*. Brockport, NY: BOA Editions.

Coles, R. (1989). *The call of stories: Teaching and the moral imagination*. Boston, MA: Houghton Mifflin.

Deng, A., Deng, B., & Ajak, B. (2005). *They poured fire on us from the sky: The true story of three lost boys from Sudan* (J. Bernstein, Ed.). New York, NY: Public Affairs.

Duncan-Andrade, J. M. R., & Morrell, E. (2008). *The art of critical pedagogy: Possibilities for moving from theory to practice in urban schools*. New York, NY: Peter Lang.

Enciso, P. E. (1994). Cultural identity and response to literature: Running lessons from Maniac Magee. *Language Arts*, 71(7), 524–533.

Fecho, B. (2004). *Is this English? Race, language, and culture in the classroom.* New York, NY: Teachers College Press.

Fecho, B. (2011a). *Teaching for the students: Habits of heart, mind, and practice in the engaged classroom.* New York, NY: Teachers College Press.

Fecho, B. (2011b). *Writing in the dialogical classroom: Students and teachers responding to the texts of their lives.* Urbana, IL: National Council of Teachers of English.

Fecho, B., & Botzakis, S. (2007). Feasts of becoming: Imagining a literacy classroom based on dialogic beliefs. *Journal of Adolescent and Adult Literacy, 50*(7), 548–558.

Fitzgerald, F. S. (1925). *The great Gatsby.* New York, NY: Scribner.

Freire, P. (1970). *Pedagogy of the oppressed.* New York, NY: Herder and Herder.

Galda, L., & Beach, R. (2001). Theory into practice: Response to literature as a cultural activity. *Reading Research Quarterly, 36*(1), 64–73.

Hafiz. (1999). Your mother and my mother. *The Gift: Poems by the great Sufi master* (D. J. Ladinsky, Trans.). New York, NY: Penguin.

Hansberry, L. (2002). *A raisin in the sun.* New York, NY: Random House.

Hermans, H., & Hermans-Konopka, A. (2010). *Dialogical self theory: Positioning and counter-positioning in a globalizing society.* Cambridge, UK: Cambridge University Press.

Hermans, H., & Kempen, H. (1993). *The dialogical self.* Toronto, Canada: Academic Press.

Himley, M., with Carini, P. F. (Eds.). (2000). *From another angle: Children's strengths and school standards.* New York, NY: Teachers College Press.

Holland, D., Lachicotte, W. Jr., Skinner, D., & Cain, C. (1998). *Identity and agency in cultural worlds.* Cambridge, MA: Harvard University Press.

Hughes, J., & Jacobson, T. (Producers), & Hughes, J. (Director). (1986). *Ferris Bueller's day off* [Motion picture]. United States: Paramount Pictures.

Jefferson, T. (1801, March 4). First inaugural address, Washington, DC. *Presidential addresses and messages* (Lit2Go ed.). Retrieved from etc.usf.edu/lit2go/132/presidential-addresses-and-messages/5163/first-inaugural-address-washington-dc-march-4-1801/_

JR. (2011). One year of turning the world inside out. *Technology, Entertainment, Design.* Retrieved from www.ted.com/talks/jr_one_year_of_turning_the_world_inside_out?language=en

Kenner, H. (1968). *The counterfeiters: An historical comedy.* London, UK: Dalkey Archive Press.

Kenner, H. (1975). *A homemade world: The American modernist writers.* Baltimore, MD: Johns Hopkins University Press.

King, A. (1993). From sage on the stage to guide on the side. *College Teaching, 41*(1), 30–35.

King, M. L., Jr. (1963a). I have a dream. Retrieved from www.archives.gov/press/exhibits/dream-speech.pdf

King, M. L., Jr. (1963b). Letter from a Birmingham jail. Retrieved from www.africa. upenn.edu/Articles_Gen/Letter_Birmingham.html

Kittle, P. (2013). *Book love: Developing depth, stamina, and passion in adolescent readers.* Portsmouth, NH: Heinemann.

Lauenstein, C., & Lauenstein, W. (Producers & Directors). (1989). *Balance* [Video file]. Germany. Retrieved from www.youtube.com/watch?v=1CTesYaduBA

Loveless, T. (2012). The 2012 Brown Center report on American education: How well are American students learning: With sections on predicting the effect of the Common Core State Standards, achievement gaps on the two NAEP tests, and misinterpreting international test scores. Retrieved from www.brookings. edu/~/media/newsletters/0216_brown_education_loveless.pdf

Miller, A. (2000). *The crucible: A play in four acts.* London, UK: Penguin Books.

Miller, D. (2009). *The book whisperer.* San Francisco, CA: Jossey Bass.

Mylan, M., & Shenk, J. (Producers & Directors). (2004). *Lost boys of Sudan* (Motion picture). United States: Actual Films.

Nafisi, A. (2005). Mysterious connections that link us together. Retrieved from www.npr.org/templates/story/story.php?storyId=4753976

National Association for the Education of Young Children. (2011). The Common Core State Standards: Caution and opportunity for early childhood education. Retrieved from www.naeyc.org/files/naeyc/11_CommonCore1_2A_rv2.pdf

National Governors Association Center for Best Practices & Council of Chief State School Officers. (2010). *Common Core State Standards.* Washington, DC: Authors.

National School Reform Faculty. (2014). NSRF protocols and activities . . . from A to Z. Retrieved from www.nsrfharmony.org/free-resources/protocols/a-z

No Child Left Behind (NCLB) Act of 2001, Pub. L. No. 107-110, § 115, Stat. 1425. (2002).

Orwell. G. (1950). *1984.* New York, NY: Signet Classic.

Palmer, P. (1998). *The courage to teach.* San Francisco, CA: Jossey-Bass.

Potok, C. (1967). *The chosen: A novel.* New York, NY: Simon and Schuster.

Sandars, N. (1972). *The epic of Gilgamesh.* New York, NY: Penguin Group.

Satir, V. (2003). Making contact. In S. M. Intrator & M. Scribner (Eds.), *Teaching with fire: Poetry that sustains the courage to teach* (pp. 122–123). San Francisco, CA: Jossey-Bass.

Snowden, D., & Boone, M. (2007). A leader's framework for decision making. *Harvard Business Review, 85*(11), 68–76.

Spiegelman, A. (1986). *Maus: A survivor's tale.* New York, NY: Pantheon Books.

Steinbeck, J. (1993). *Of mice and men.* New York, NY: Penguin Books.

Tanen, N., & Hughes, J. (Producers), & Hughes, J. (Director). (1985). *The breakfast club* [Motion picture]. United States: Universal Studios.

Wiesel, E. (1999, April 12). The perils of indifference: Lessons learned from a violent century. Speech presented at Millennium Evening in the East Room of the White House, Washington, DC. Retrieved from www.pbs.org/eliewiesel/resources/ millennium.htmlcritical

Wiesel, E. (2000). *Night.* Norwalk, CT: Easton Press.

Index

About the Contributors

Ian Altman grew up in Macon, Georgia, and Cincinnati, Ohio. He has degrees from the University of Georgia in philosophy and in language and literacy education. Ian has been an English teacher at Clarke Central High School since 2006 and English department chair since 2010. He serves on the Clarke County School District's Teacher Advisory Board, the UGA College of Education's Board of Visitors, and the Georgia Conflict Center's Board of Advisors. Ian also volunteers for Athens U-Lead, mentoring immigrant students through the college and scholarship application process.

Paige Cole is lucky enough to live in Athens, Georgia, with her husband, Toby, and teach social studies at North Oconee High School. When she is not teaching or working in the community with young people, you can find her running, performing live band karaoke, practicing yoga, or walking little terriers with underbites. Now that she has finished a PhD from the University of Georgia in language and literacy, she strives for time to read fiction, takes pleasure in friends and family, and tries to be less pushy. Her next project deals with teaching climate change for the selfish reason of wanting to be able to complete section hiking the Appalachian Trail when she retires.

Angela Dean has completed her 13th year of teaching secondary language arts to both 9th- and 10th-graders. This year, Angela was nominated for teacher of the year and was named one of the top three finalists. She received her BSED in Language and Literacy Education from the University of Georgia in 2002. She returned to UGA for her MEd in language and literacy education and completed the degree in 2007. Angela works closely with and is a proud teacher consultant for the Red Clay Writing Project. Through her involvement with the Red Clay Writing Project, Angela has been part of several teacher research projects that have led to publications. Angela enjoys traveling and seeing live music with her husband, Andy Dean. They live in Athens, Georgia, with their three dogs.

Michelle Falter is a doctoral candidate in the Department of Language and Literacy Education at the University of Georgia and former editor of the *Journal of Language and Literacy Education*. She has been a secondary English teacher for 10 years, having the privilege of teaching in both the United States and abroad, in the Dominican Republic and Germany. Michelle's scholarship focuses on the role of emotion in the classroom and helping educators co-construct knowledge with their students using participatory, critical, and dialogical teaching practices.

Bob Fecho is a professor of English education at Teachers College, Columbia University, where his work has focused on issues of language, identity, sociocultural perspectives, and dialogical pedagogy as they relate to adolescent literacy among marginalized populations. He is also founding director of the Red Clay Writing Project at the University of Georgia. His recent books, *Teaching for the Students: Habits of Heart, Mind, and Practice in the Engaged Classroom* (Teachers College Press, 2011) and *Writing in the Dialogical Classroom: Students and Teachers Responding to the Texts of Their Lives* (NCTE, 2011) provide insight into how to teach in dialogical ways within the constraints of schools dominated by standardization.

Allisa Abraham Hall is a 10th- and 11th-grade English instructor specializing in choice reading instruction, and a doctoral candidate in language and literacy education at the University of Georgia. Her poems have been published in *JoLLE* and *English Journal*.

Xiaoli Hong is a doctoral candidate at the University of Georgia in the Department of Language and Literacy Education. Her research interests include multicultural children's literature, children's response to literature, and family literacy practices.